THE NIGHT BEGINS WITH A QUESTION

THE NIGHT BEGINS WITH A QUESTION

XXV Austrian Poems
1978-2002

Edited by Iain Galbraith

CARCANET

SCOTTISH POETRY LIBRARY

By leaves we live

First published in 2007 by

The Scottish Poetry Library
5 Crichton's Close
Canongate
Edinburgh
EH8 8DT

and

Carcanet Press Limited
Alliance House
Cross Street
Manchester
M2 7AQ

Introduction and this selection © 2007 Iain Galbraith
Editorial concept © Scottish Poetry Library
Individual poems © the authors and translators; the acknowledgements
on p.103 constitute an extension of this copyright page.

ISBN 1 85754 915 5

The publishers gratefully acknowledge support from the Scottish Arts Council
and the Kunstsektion des Bundeskanzleramts (Austria) towards the publication
of this title.

Designed and typeset by Barrie Tullett in Shaker

Printed and bound by
elpeeko of Lincoln, UK

Supported by
The National Lottery®
through the Scottish Arts Council

Scottish
Arts Council

BUNDESKANZLERAMT ▪ KUNST

Contents

Editorial Note

This selection was made on the principal of one poem per year. The poem may have appeared in a magazine or a collection published during that year. Publication details appear with the poets' biographies at the end of the book.

I would like to extend my thanks to everyone involved in this publication, particularly Iain Galbraith who accepted the challenge of choosing twenty-five poems, and is a meticulous editor of texts both original and translated; the translators Iain Bamforth, Ron Butlin, Regi Claire, Ken Cockburn, Iain Galbraith and Angus Reid for their creative responses; Dr Johannes Wimmer of the Austrian Cultural Forum (London) for his encouragement and support; and to all those at the Scottish Poetry Library and Carcanet Press who have helped to bring this project to fruition.

Robyn Marsack
Series Editor

Introduction

The early modern English word utopia, translated 'back' into the Greek from which its parts were drawn, would mean 'no place/land', and the topics of 'de-territorialization' and fragmentary identity are ones in which post-1945 Austrian literature is rich. To offer a trivial example: these pages are written in the final days of 2006, the year in which the Austrians celebrated the 250th birthday of their most celebrated son, baptised Joannes Chrysostomus Wolfgangus Theophilus Mozart. But was Mozart really Austrian? The facts say that Mozart was born in the Archbishopric of Salzburg in 1756, which first became part of Austria in 1805, 13 years years after Mozart's death. This, of course, is the stuff of wise-cracks, and the reader may be assured of my sympathy for his or her impatient rejoinder: 'Well, if he wasn't Austrian then, he certainly is now!'

But the conundrum of Mozart's un-Austrian birth is symptomatic of a more general Austrian malaise with the fraught question of birthright and belonging: historically speaking, many of 'Old Austria's' writers, if we gauged their nationalities by state borders post-dating those of the Habsburg Empire, could be seen today as Russian, Polish, Rumanian, Slovenian, Czech, Slovakian, German, Hungarian, Italian, or indeed, in the meantime, as having belonged to several different nationalities. If Scotland has been seen as a 'nation without a state', then the Second Austrian Republic, it has been said, is 'a state without a history', or – more attractively, if the nettle is grasped – with many histories. In one sense, then, its heritage of a diversity of fragmented, multicultural traditions might be thought to place modern Austria at the forefront of global developments in a world in which the nineteenth-century dream/nightmare of a unified national tradition, to which Austria's post-war leadership aspired, offers little to sustain human (or humane) survival in the 21st century. But if post-war Austria has become an independent state, the people who live there cannot gain independence from Austria's several histories. The title of one of Robert Schindel's volumes of poetry is *Ohneland* (Without Land), and the implied enforced utopia, leaving the embittered subject of Schindel's 'Homeland Romance' to echo some of the bleaker cadences of – among other poems – Hölderlin's 'Half of Life', marks post-war Austria's failure for several decades to seriously 'inherit' the consequences of its seven years of complicity in National Socialism. A selective heritage, one that ignores the era of Austrian history during which members of Schindel's family were deported to concentration camps, must lead to the state of 'landlessness' addressed in his poem. For Schindel, in a poem entitled 'Vineta I', Vienna is 'the most beautiful city in the world, right by the river Lethe': what once was the 'world-capital of anti-Semitism' has become the 'capital of forgetting'. For Hölderlin's Hyperion too, 'Heimat' (home) had distanced itself from the poets, leaving them 'strangers in their own home'. Many of the poems in this anthology bear witness to this condition in one way or another: Heidi Pataki's eponymous 'angel' is torn between a social diaspora and dreams of destruction; Andreas Okopenko's dream-log mountineer finds his surroundings 'don't exactly' fill him 'with joy'; Peter Rosei's narrator is a volubly distanced, ironic observer; the subject of the South Tyrolean norbert c. kaser's poem wishes for a home he wouldn't feel impelled to leave, while Oswald Egger, also from the semi-autonomous region of South Tyrol, seems intent on an encyclopaedic re-incorporation of the world as it unfolds. A ruptured, yet familiar landscape is inhabited with intensely painful sensuality in Ilse Aichinger's prose poem 'Connecting Train', from which the present anthology takes its title, and where the railway line referred to is the one along which the poet's grandmother and other relatives were deported to Minsk and their deaths in the Shoah.

Poetry, for all the contingencies of its makers and materials, nevertheless persists in a dimension that is uniquely unhinged to time and space. Poets are anachronistic listeners, heedful of the rhythms of absent voices, solicitous of the intervals and shifts in breathing that carry across births, deaths, empires and centuries. Drawn to the architecture of a rare but commonable medium, whose incumbent presences and insistent demands may have roots in different languages and on distant continents, poets are the heirs to a continuum, participation in whose auditory and visual conference depends on the poet's alertness – when it seems there is too much noise and too little time to listen – to the fine-tuning of instruments shaped and strung by successive generations of inventors, deconstructors, revealers and re-arrangers. Such colloquies are for the greater part less than explicit, yet they account, perhaps, for the paradoxical strain of contemporaneity that will enter a dialogue between poets of very different eras: in this anthology, between Erich Fried and Georg Trakl, Ferdinand Schmatz and Osip Mandelstam, Robert Schindel and Friedrich Hölderlin, or Ingeborg Bachmann and the fragment of a stage direction, heading Act III/ Scene 3 of William Shakespeare's *A Winter's Tale*, which entered her mind on a journey to Prague in 1964.

Poetry's council of echoes will inevitably be a theme in any verse anthology. The present selection includes a number of very fine, if very different love poems (by Evelyn Schlag, Alfred Kolleritsch, Reinhard Priessnitz, Julian Schutting, Franzobel, Andreas Okopenko and others), and, as a reader, one is frequently aware of the way the apparent subject of a poem may be interwoven with poetry's own groundswell of resonances (Schlag), exchanges (Schutting), searchings (Priessnitz), in-streamings (Kolleritsch), dreams (Okopenko) and messages (Franzobel). Between what is perhaps little more than a bodily 'lurch' – a metabolic 'surge', intent on urging a writer's arm 'to tryst the wrist' and 'the pencil's hand' – and that moment when 'the letters' circle, dove-winged, rises' (Ferdinand Schmatz), lies the struggle for poetic translation into whatever language, or plurality of languages, may be present. For the unmade poem can appear to arise 'from the rubble of what froths up' (Franz Josef Czernin). Such incidental matter might consist of 'a thonet chair at the edge of the lake' (H. C. Artmann), the coincidence of 'apple, front door, glass of milk' and 'boot' (Peter Waterhouse), or even 'something breathing .../something scarcely perceptible bestirring itself/something irregular/all wrinkled up!' (Friederike Mayröcker). The face discovered in Mayröcker's poem, framed in the reflecting surface and surprisingly consummate among the quotidian detail of a life, is as strange and distant as it is instantly recognizable. As the site of a transaction 'between two/ ages', the poem is finally made – but the glance at the mirror catches something that is hauntingly ambivalent.

This 'art' of poetic translation necessarily stretches a poet's sensibility across debatable lands (which, as I have already suggested, are legion in Austrian history). The subject of Michael Donhauser's poem, positioned 'as one who stands beside his bag in the/dust', has come to find that he belongs to a 'lost land', heavy with death and beginnings. The 'slope-/stretched meadows' of Christoph Wilhelm Aigner's poem seem the tense ciphers of an erotic yearning; the word 'bird' in Raoul Schrott's 'Physikalische Optik I', mysteriously come 'out of November' to reveal its vestigial gravity on an Innsbruck balcony, suggests an opening to a new and investigative perspective (Raoul Schrott's poem stands at the beginning of his outstanding collection *Tropen*); the 'blind skin of the ancestors', on the other hand, threatening to suffocate the anxious subject of Ernst Jandl's grotesque 'swiss army knife', incorporates an equally pressing, nightmarish side to this dialogue between ages. Perforation of that hooded integument may free the gaze only to 'look/out of the terror/into the eternal darkness'. Maja Haderlap's Carinthian-Slovenian 'song', too, 'as though from somewhere else insists', and yet the traditions it receives and must partly reject are 'a history/transport of transparent stumps' – something it is better to 'unlearn', a process which may itself require 'time to go wrecking'.

In Marie-Thérèse Kerschbaumer's poem the debatable lands are war-divided, and the breathless echoes she has captured of 'four hundred children' in mortal peril in 1939 are muted and broken by a snow-blanket covering of English reportage, sifted by the poet in the Viennese Documents Archive of the Austrian Resistance.

In Erich Fried's poem, 'Trakl-Haus', it is the oppressive weight of history that drives the young Georg Trakl 'pell-mell through narrow lanes' into 'dream and disarray'. Inherited structures here present themselves as the 'petrifactions of death'. Like the Jews 'driven out' of Trakl's Salzburg, Fried's early life was marred by the persecution and murder of members of his family, by the grievous loss of both his father Hugo, who died as a consequence of Gestapo interrogation, and his 'fatherland', Austria. Forced to flee from Vienna and the Nazis in 1938, Fried spent the rest of his life in London, where his kindness to exiled writers was proverbial, and where his house became a meeting place for German and Austrian writers until many years after the war. (It was under Fried's roof that Michael Hamburger first met Paul Celan, for example, prompting Hamburger's translations of Celan's poetry.)

It was in London, too, in her Kensington hotel in 1967, that Erich Fried discussed the present anthology's opening poem 'Böhmen liegt am Meer' ('Bohemia, a Country by the Sea') with its author, Ingeborg Bachmann. His account of that meeting contains a passage that seems of particular usefulness to any explanation of Austrian poetic weights and measures. Here Fried remembers calling Bachmann's attention to her elision of vocalic verb endings in the poem, a tendency remarkable even in phrases where there was no need to avoid a hiatus between vowels, no obvious advantage to the cadence of a line. He goes on to remind her that such typically Austrian elisions had been commoner in her early poems, but that she had later adapted her orthography to comply with what he ironically refers to as 'pan-German' literary standards. Bachmann's reply to Fried's implication that she had returned to Austrian usage was to explain that the condition described in the poem made it no longer necessary to comply in that way, and that her mode of expression therefore 'corresponded to the content of the poem'. The question inevitably arises as to what the 'condition described in the poem' might be. While this short introduction cannot be the place to interpret one of Ingeborg Bachmann's most influential and memorable poems – the poem Franz-Josef Murau, 'hero' of Thomas Bernhard's novel *Auslöschung* (Extinction), calls 'so Austrian, but at the same time so permeated by the whole world, and by the world surrounding this world' – it is nonetheless useful to know that the poem's first drafts were written while Bachmann was travelling to Vienna, via 'Bohemian' Prague, from Berlin. Her visit to Berlin, by her own account, had been traumatic – 'the most tortured state I ever got into in any country'. There were probably several reasons for that 'tortured state'. If the word 'trauma' may be used with any exactitude here, then because her encounter with the former capital city of Nazi terror – far from causing her to veer from standard German and dig in her local heels, falling back on the 'elisions' of a comforting Austrian home place – had confronted her with impressions and perceptions which – corresponding to those of her childhood in the Austria of the Nazi years – triggered suppressed memories and suggested 'links which had previously eluded her grasp' (Sigrid Weigel). In this condition of being 'at sea', knowing the world 'from rock-bottom' was a prerequisite to gaining 'sight' of her 'chosen land', a land neither Austrian nor German, but 'bordering' on all countries and all languages: utopian, and tragically brimming with promise.

The blueprint for this book was drawn by Ken Cockburn and Robyn Marsack in their anthology *Intimate Expanses. XXV Scottish Poems 1978-2002*, and while I have been happy to follow the principle of one poem per year, I should point out that two of the poems are linked to their years by dates of composition rather than publication. The compact nature of this selection has inevitably meant I have been unable to include poets who have an equal claim to be represented here: I shall mention only Erwin Einzinger, Elfriede Gerstl, Bettina Balàka, Antonio Fian, Gustav Janus, Klaus Demus and Cvetka Lipuš. Anthologies by their very nature involve the work of many people, and I would like to acknowledge my gratitude here to the many authors who have answered my queries, to the translators for their sensitivity and erudition, to Valerie Besl for opening the archives of the Haymon Verlag, to Rainer Götz for opening his address book, to Heinz Bachmann for his good offices, to Thomas Eder and Ferdinand Schmatz for access to the Priessnitz Archive, to the staff of the Scottish Poetry Library, and especially to Robyn Marsack for her extraordinary patience and helpful suggestions.

Iain Galbraith
Wiesbaden, December 2006

THE POEMS

Böhmen liegt am Meer

Sind hierorts Häuser grün, tret ich noch in ein Haus.
Sind hier die Brücken heil, geh ich auf gutem Grund.
Ist Liebesmüh in alle Zeit verloren, verlier ich sie hier gern.

Bin ich's nicht, ist es einer, der ist so gut wie ich.

Grenzt hier ein Wort an mich, so laß ich's grenzen.
Liegt Böhmen noch am Meer, glaub ich den Meeren wieder.
Und glaub ich noch ans Meer, so hoffe ich auf Land.

Bin ich's, so ist's ein jeder, der ist soviel wie ich.
Ich will nichts mehr für mich. Ich will zugrunde gehn.

Zugrund – das heißt zum Meer, dort find ich Böhmen wieder.
Zugrund gerichtet, wach ich ruhig auf.
Von Grund auf weiß ich jetzt, und ich bin unverloren.

Kommt her, ihr Böhmen alle, Seefahrer, Hafenhuren und Schiffe
unverankert. Wollt ihr nicht böhmisch sein, Illyrer, Veroneser,
und Venezianer alle. Spielt die Komödien, die lachen machen

Und die zum Weinen sind. Und irrt euch hundertmal,
wie ich mich irrte und Proben nie bestand,
dort hab ich sie bestanden, ein um das andere Mal.

Wie Böhmen sie bestand und eines schönen Tags
ans Meer begnadigt wurde und jetzt am Wasser liegt.

Ich grenz noch an ein Wort und an ein andres Land,
ich grenz, wie wenig auch, an alles immer mehr,

ein Böhme, ein Vagant, der nichts hat, den nichts hält,
begabt nur noch, vom Meer, das strittig ist, Land meiner Wahl zu sehen.

1978 | Ingeborg Bachmann

Bohemia, a Country by the Sea

If houses hereabouts are green, I'll cross the threshold again;
the bridges safe and sound, I'll walk on solid ground.
If love's a labour lost for ever, I'm glad to squander it here.

If I'm not the one, then someone else will do just as well.

If a word here lies beside me, it'll be my borderline.
If Bohemia's still a country by the sea, I can believe in the sea again.
And still believing in the sea, I can hope for land.

If I'm the one it could be anyone at all, anyone as much as me.
There's nothing that I want. I want to go under.

Go under – towards the sea, where I'll find Bohemia again.
Sundered and wrecked, to wake up peacefully.
To know things from rock-bottom, and no longer count for lost.

Come, fair Bohemians, all you sailors, whores and ships
without a mooring. Won't you be Bohemian, you Illyrians, Veronese
and Venetians too. Put on those comedies that make us laugh

and those that are passing sad. Go astray a hundred times,
just as I went astray and never once passed muster,
though I withstood the trials, from the first to the very last.

Withstood them like Bohemia which, one fine day,
was pardoned to the sea and now takes up the shore.

Still I border on a word and on another country,
verging more closely, if never very much, on what exists,

a penniless Bohemian, a vagabond without ties,
my sole talent to be at sea at the sight of my chosen land.

translated by Iain Bamforth | 1978

die laerche

gerne waer ich eine laerche
mueßte nicht trinken
nix rauchen
nicht mich brauchen
zu bewegen
nur bewegen lassen

gerne waer ich eine laerche
im schnee
ohne gewand
& saeh uebers land
im fruehjahr
laerchengruen

nur bewegen lassen
von boden regen hagel
(eller)
wind

gerne auch aelter
wuerd ich werrn
denn
sie

afers 280578

1979 | norbert c. kaser

the larch

I'd like to be a larch
wouldn't have to drink
or smoke
wouldn't need
to move
just let myself be moved

I'd like to be a larch
in the snow
without garments
& would see across the land
in the spring
larch-green

just let myself be moved
by ground rain hail
(eller)
wind

I'd like to get
older too
than
it

afers 280578

translated by Ron Butlin and Regi Claire | 1979

von damals an

beim Erwachen
im dunklen Fensterausschnitt
ein riesiger
blanker im Rollen funkelnder
Stern

etwas Atmendes, rufe ich
etwas kaum wahrnehmbar sich Regendes
etwas ungleichmäszig
Zerknittertes!
eine schwarze Schleife am Mantelärmel der Mutter

im Krankenhaus,
am sechsten August,
etwas kaum Atmendes
etwas kaum merkbar Knitterndes,
eine schwarze Seidenblume im Ausschnitt des Kleides der Mutter
etwas Atmendes
ganz ungleichmäszig –
der wahre Kunsttrieb
Kunst des Geschlechts

zwischen zwei
Altern, hinter dem Pult, die Frau
mit dem Perlencollier,
Imitation Nachbildung, minder-
wertiges TRAUMSCHNEIDEN, so
habe er gern
die Bedeutung von Wörtern
nachgeschlagen,
Kanapee, rigoros, Brevier – –
aber das Foto! rufe ich,
er atmet auf diesem Foto!

1980 | Friederike Mayröcker

since then

on awakening
in the dark of the windowpane
a sheer enormous
star
glittering in motion

something breathing, I exclaim
something scarcely perceptible bestirring itself
something irregular
all wrinkled up!
a black ribbon on the sleeve of my mother's coat

in the hospital,
on the sixth of August,
something scarcely breathing
something that hardly appears to be rustling,
a black silk flower on the neckline of my mother's dress
something breathing
most irregularly –
the true impulse to make art
a sex-specific art

between two
ages, behind the desk, the woman
with the pearl necklace,
imitation copy, low-
value DREAM EDITING, oh yes
he was always keen
on poring over
the meaning of words,
settee, adamant, breviary –
but that photo! I exclaim,
he's breathing in this photo!

translated by Iain Bamforth | 1980

ganz wenig,
hamsterbackig,
ein Stück Brotrinde zwischen Zähnen und Wange,
mein Spiegelbild an diesem Morgen,
en face
linksseitig,
rechts :
aus dem Gebrauch heraus.

für meinen Vater

very little,
him with his hamster cheeks,
a bit of crust between teeth and cheek,
the face I saw in the mirror today,
en face,
from the left-hand side,
then the right :
no longer in the habit.

for my father

translated by Iain Bamforth | 1980

angel esterminador

aus den lokalen fliegt er raus; er putzt die klinken
dem würgeengel gehts ganz jämmerlich
wenn er sich seine kuttelsuppe kocht

oder im supermarkt so tut, als wollt er katzenfutter
in konserven tatsächlich kaufen für die katz, und meilenweit
nach pisse stinkt, die tüten aus den abfalleimern klaubt

das graue haar ihm wirr zu berge steht, wenn er mit lumpen
an den füßen die treppen hochkeucht, schnüffeln
die nachbarn, schütteln sich vor ekel

es gibt so viele neue schreckgespenster!
nicht mal im wahlkampf hat er was verloren
nachts, wenn er auf den metrostufen schnarcht:

wie elendig bin ich am tag, unnütz & ohne arbeit!
im traum ein schwerer vogel, dessen schwingen rauschen
ach, immer so über der erde schweben können!

die tiefen dunkeln wasser unten in der tiefe
die dunkeln tiefen lüfte oben in der luft
zerschnitten durch das netz der leitungsdrähte

hochspannungsmaste, ach! an sie zu rühren
den blitz zu lösen, daß der funke glüht
und mein verheerter leib durch radarschirme

als asche oder schatten auf die erde sinkt...
so will ich gern zu staub zerfallen:
die großen schiffe schaukeln weiter auf den meeren

öltanker, dampfer und containerfrachter
im flug ein hellerleuchtetes café mit billiardspielern
und klitzeklein die alten leute in den liegestühlen

1981 | Heidi Pataki

angel esterminador

he gets chucked out of pubs; he goes begging
the angel of death is in bad shape
when he cooks himself some tripe

or, at the supermarket, pretends he wants to buy tinned
cat food really for the cat, and stinks of piss
for miles, scavenges from litter bins

his grey hair tangled and on end, when he pants
up the stairs with rags on his feet, the neighbours
sniff, shudder in disgust

there are so many new bogeymen!
he's not wanted – not even in election campaigns
when he snores at night on the steps of the metro:

how wretched I am by day, useless & idle!
in dreams a heavy bird whose wings swish
oh, to hover like this above the earth forever!

the deep dark waters down below
the dark deep skies up above
criss-crossed by wires

electricity pylons, oh! to touch them
to release the lightning so the spark glows
and my destroyed body's scattered across radar screens

as ash or shadow onto the earth…
thus I'd willingly crumble to dust:
the big ships continue jogging across the seas

oil tankers, steamboats and containerships
in flight a brightly lit café with billiard players
and, teensy-weensy, the old people in their deck chairs

translated by Ron Butlin and Regi Claire | 1981

sich wiegend, dösend, zeitunglesend, der kanari pfeift
dann ein grellroter pummeliger wagen, altes fordmodell
unter der brücke auf der autobahn, und drüber weiße wölkchen

rocking, dozing, reading the paper, the budgie sings
then a gaudy-red chubby car, an old Ford
under the motorway bridge, and above it little white clouds

translated by Ron Butlin and Regi Claire | 1981

Trakl-Haus, Salzburg

Zu schwer das Gewölbe:
ein Albtraum
dunkel und schön
in der schönen Stadt
zu stark und zu unverfallen
um zu hoffen auf ein Erwachen
zu alt um in ihm zu leben
zu alt um in ihm zu wohnen
und leben zu bleiben
in kühlen Zimmern ohne Sinn
Zu schön um sich
beizeiten von ihm zu trennen

Gänge und Mauern
sind Knochen des steinernen Todes
Ein eiserner Vater
half diesen Steinen keltern
den einsamen Sohn
und ihn pressen in frühen Herbst
Engel mit kalten Stirnen
trugen Verwesung

Und aus dem Haus
fliehend durch enge Gassen
durch das finstere Neutor unter dem Mönchsberg
sah er drohen von oben
die Feste Hohensalzburg
die Zwingburg die
die Juden vertrieben hat
die Bauern geknechtet hat
die Salzknappen besiegt hat
Wo war da Freiheit
außer in Traum und Umnachtung?

1982 | Erich Fried

Trakl-Haus, Salzburg

Too weighty the arches:
a mountain of the mind
dark and beautiful
in the beautiful city
too solid and too undilapidated
for any hope of an awakening
too old to live in
too old to dwell in
and remain alive
in cool rooms bereft of meaning
Too splendid to leave
in proper time

Passageways and walls
are the petrifactions of death
An iron father
helped this wine-stone press
the lonely son
and release him to early autumn
Angels with cold foreheads
were dressed in decay

And from the house
pell-mell through narrow lanes
through the sinister Neutor under the Mönchsberg
he saw looming from above
the fortress Hohensalzburg
the stronghold which had
driven the Jews out
enslaved the farmers
triumphed over the salt-workers
Where was freedom then
except in dream and disarray?

translated by Iain Bamforth | 1982

schweizer armeemesser

warum so viele tage, wenn
so wenig ich erinnern kann
von ihnen allen. krachend schlagen
die türen zu, o du gnadenloser
sturm. meine sittiche
flattern schreiend um meinen kopf
und ich perforiere
mit meinem schweizer armeemesser
die blinde haut der vorfahren
die sich über meine zuckende
gestalt will wickeln,
daß meinen augen doch
noch bleibe ein loch, um hinaus
aus dem schrecken zu gucken
in die ewige finsternis

1983 | Ernst Jandl

swiss army knife

why so many days when
I can remember so little
of them all. with a crash
the doors bang shut, oh you pitiless
storm. my budgies
flutter screaming round my head
and I perforate
with my swiss army knife
the blind skin of the ancestors
that wants to wind itself
around my writhing figure,
so there may still remain
a hole for my eyes to look
out of the terror
into the eternal darkness

translated by Ron Butlin and Regi Claire | 1983

vierhundert kinder im schnee

vierhundert kinder aus sicherem tod
französische infanterie siebentausend fuß erklomm-/pyrenäen/
ein zug eine ganze kompanie/
oh so deep/oh so schmal// wie gewunden/pitfalls
waten drei meter tief/scheewächten durch/ten feet deep
vierhundert kinder und einhundertfünfzig frauen/nachts/
die infanteristen den col d'aras
schneeschuhe und schlitten/aufbruch und aufstieg/zur –
danach acht stunden/die zerstörte kapelle ein schelter –
wenig frauen/ and practically none of the children could walk
der französische innenminister eilte an die grenze und sah zu
wie sich die katalonischen kinder am mahl erfreuten das/
(für sie zubereitet war)
wenn die nationalisten vorrücken/werden zwanzigtausend
unglücklichen/schrecklichen hänge erklommen/schneebedeckten
nach puigcerda hinaufströmen/bergpfade/und/weitere zwanzigtausend
militiamen too.
und diese horden/die grenzen überfluten/ein offizier
diese verzweifelten/bewaffneten wanderer
und so wurden sie umzingelt und in gewahrsam genommen.
die milizen und die einsamen plätze
übergänge und verschwiegene hütten.
dann/sie/die hütten/anzünden wollten/die voll heu waren.
die hungernde masse verbrachte die nacht auf durchweichten feldern
in gräben und auf lastwägen/and this hardship they are undergoing.

(wien, 11. märz 1984)

four hundred children in the snow

four hundred children from certain death
french infantry climbed seven thousand feet /pyrenees/
a platoon a whole company/
oh so deep/oh so narrow//how winding/*pitfalls*
wade three metres deep/ through snowdrifts /*ten feet deep*
four hundred children and one hundred and fifty women/at night/
the infantrymen the col d'aras
snowshoes and sledges/departure and ascent/to –
afterwards eight hours/the destroyed chapel a shelter –
few women/*and practically none of the children could walk*
the french interior minister rushed to the border to watch
the catalan children enjoy the meal that/
(had been prepared for them)
when the nationalists advance/twenty thousand will
unfortunates/having climbed terrible hillsides/snow-covered
stream up to puigcerda/mountain paths/and/a further twenty-thousand
militiamen too.
and these hordes/will flood the borders/an officer
these desperate/armed wanderers
and so they were surrounded and taken into custody.
the militia and the lonely places
crossings and secluded huts.
then/they/wanted to set fire to/the huts/which were full of hay.
the starving masses spent the night in soggy fields
in trenches and on lorries/*and this hardship they are undergoing.*

(vienna, 11 march 1984)

translated by Ron Butlin and Regi Claire | 1984

Salerno

warum nicht, wenn es sein müßte
und du dergleichen überhaupt zuließest,
den Motor eines Tieres,
für uns zu sterben gewohnt,
würde das
für dich um sein Herz Gebrachte
in und mit dem
an dich verlorenen Herzen
in dir weiterleben so lange wie du,

warum nicht ausgetauscht bekommen,
was ja nur ein Muskel ist
und nicht die Seele,
in der die Liebe zu Dir wohnt,
auch der neue
würde seiner ruhigen Bewegung
ihre Bewegheit übertragen lassen,
als wäre er
dies flutend
Deinem Herzen Sich-weiten

warum nicht, liebes Herz,
Deinetwegen hin und wieder
Urwaldaffen-
herzzerspringen
und nach kleine Herz-
losigkeiten
eine Nacht lang Schweineherzweh!

1985 | Julian Schutting

Salerno

why not, if it had to be
and you were prepared to take it on,
the motor of an animal,
accustomed to dying on our behalf,
that the animal
robbed of its heart for your sake
in and with the heart
lost to you
would live on in as long as you,

why not have replaced what is
after all only a muscle
and not the soul,
in which love lives at home with you,
even the new one
would carry love's fluster
over into its calm movement,
as if it would
flood and dilate
your selfhood heartwards

why not, now and then,
because of you, sweetheart,
primate
explosions of the heart
and after minor acts of heart-
lessness
a whole night's *nostalgie de la boue*!

translated by Iain Bamforth | 1985

Hauptstadt der Sprache

Wir zerrisssen, und die Sprache war da. Viele Wörter. Wie
als Apfel, Haustür, Glas Milch darf ich sein? O
ihr Straßenbahnen. Besserer Bus. Ein Stiefel
ist mehr Schuh als ich. Schuhwerk.
Ich falle als Apfel aus meinem Bett. Die Sprache war da.
Socken angezogen. Wo ist das, welches eher Schuh ist als ich?
Mit vielen Wörtern geht man auf die Straße und sieht doch
sehr still aus. Lautes Automobil ist wunderbar still.
Fahrende Sprechblase. Die Sprache, Sprachel. Spreks.
Der Sprachling. Der Sprachling mit dem Schuhling
als gehende Haustür, die hinter uns zuschlägt. Alles als Tür
weit geöffnet, geschlossen. Ein Licht ist das Wort
unter dem wir gehen. Es ist das Licht
wie es uns nicht zerriß: Apfel im Mund
Füße im Schuh: so machen wir auf und zu.
Das Licht auf der Straße heißt in der Bahn eine nachtlose Fahrt.
Viele Wörter sind nahtlos. Wir leben mit Haustüren
oder Haustieren. Die Wolken fahren als sehr große.
Viele Wörter: wir rennen damit auseinander, mit dem Apfel
zur Tür und mit uns hinaus. Und die Sprache war da.
Wir wohnen in sehr vielen Häusern. Namen der Großstädte.
Der Bus ist eine Stadt in der Stadt. Schuhwerk.
Schuhwerk war da. Hinter der geschlossenen Tür
ist die Hauptstraße eine Vergangenheit. Und die Sprache war da
wir zerrissen. Viele Wörter
wir sind viele. Hauptstadt der Schuhe. Meine Haustiere
sind Katzen als Schuhe. Man geht nahtlos auf die Straße.
Straße war da. Ich renne im Licht. Licht war da.
Hauptstadt der Sprache: hunderttausendmal heißt der Apfel: bitte
ein Kilogramm Äpfel.
Nahtlose Äpfel sind viele Wörter. Die Stadt springt am Ort auseinander.
Die Gasse ist ein Haustor als viele. Die eigene Türe ist die Türe des Nachbarn
als andere. Guten Tag. Viele Wörter. Hauptstadt der anderen.

1986 | Peter Waterhouse

Capital of Language

We tore and language was there. Lots of words. How
apple, front door, glass of milk may I be? O
you trams. Better sort of bus. A boot
is more shoe than I. Footwear.
I fall out of bed an apple. Language was here.
Socks, pulled on. Where's what's more shoe than I?
One enters the street with a lot of words and looks
really quiet. A loud automobile is wonderfully quiet.
A moving speech-bubble. The language. Langwij. Lang
wedge. The widgling. The widgling with the shoeling
as a walking front door, banging behind us. Everything
as a wide open door, closed. A light is the word
we walk under. It is the light
such as we were not torn: apple in mouth,
foot in shoe: thus we open and close too.
The seem of street lighting is a nightless trip in the tram.
Lots of words are seamless. We live with front doors
or dormice. Clouds passing by are big ones.
Lots of words: we rush apart with them, with the apple
to the door and out with us. And language was there.
We live in lots of houses. The names of the cities.
The bus is a town in town. Footwork.
Footwear was here. Behind the closed door
the high street is a past. And language was here
we torn. Lots of words
we are lots. Capital of shoes. My door mice
are cats as shoes. Seamlessly we enter the street.
Street was here. I rush in the light. Light was here.
Capital of language: the apple, a hundred thousand times as:

a kilo of apples, please.

Seamless apples are lots of words. The town in place cracks open.
The street is one front gate as lots. One's own door is the neighbour's
as another. Good morning. Lots of words. Capital of the others.

translated by Iain Galbraith | 1986

Heimatromanze

oder

Friedenslitanei Heimat Nacht Natur
(Pour Hölderlin 11)

Landloses Begreifen. Hängen im Geäst
Unter den Peitschen an beiden Armen
Aber aufgerissen im Arsch und fest
Tauchet das Abendlicht dieses Ichnest
In die Heimat Nacht. Beim Dritten Erbarmen
In der Mitte des Lebens beginnen zu reifen
Die Fröste, die Nebel, die Nebelstreifen
Hängt alles im Astwerk, das Morgenlicht lässt
Alle Peitschen als Flöten glänzend umgarnen
Sodass um das Ichnest herum Gedanken schweifen.
Unübersehbar hocket die Heimatnacht im Gesträuch und benässt
Ihre Halme und Disteln, welche einst an den Trillerpfeifen
Des peitschenschwingenden Westwinds erstarrten, ihre steifen
Nächtlichen Grünungen warn von ihm gegens Astwerk gepresst
Suchten Zuflucht im Arsch bei den plötzlichen Abendalarmen.
So hängt alles im Astwerk, als dort sich die Ichnester häufen
Idyllen im verhangenen Abend. Ein zufriednes Gebrest
Mit den Nebeln aus Endzeit hockt bäuchlings im Warmen.
Jetzt Flöten im Licht in der Frühe, als ob ein Gedächtnisrest
Zum Gedächtnis wächst unten im betauten Gesträuch. Verseifen, verseifen!
Schnell machet aus Gedächtnis Seifen, durchs Kraut die Gendarmen
Mit verknüppelten Flöten und ausklingenden Peitschen aus Ost und West
Schnalzen den Arsch in den Bauch in das Ich, vergesset, vergesst!
Allumher klirren die Fahnen, zusammengeschossene Namen schleifen
Im Sterben noch eine Wildspur, als wollten sie warnen
Die Idyllen im Astwerk droben, die atemlos und im Zusammenkneifen
Das Vierte Erbarmen erreichen wolln seis als Buchstabe seis als
Buchstabenpest

1987 | Robert Schindel

Homeland Romance

or

Peace Litany, Ground Night Nature
(For Hölderlin 11)

Realization of landlessness. To hang in the boughs
Beneath the whips by both arms
But with the shit worked out of you and fast
Fades the evening light of this me-nest
Into Night the ground of belonging. At the Third Compassion
In the middle of life begin to ripen
The frosts, the mists, the layers of mist
Everything hangs in the branches, the morning light makes
All the whips gleam beguilingly flute-like
So that around the me-nest spin roving thoughts.
Conspicuously crouches the ground of Night in the thicket and moistens
Its blades and thistles which formerly, at the pea-whistle trill
Of the whip-wielding zephyr, stiffened, her hard
Nocturnal greenings were pressed by it against the branches
Sought shelter up shit creek at the sudden evening alarms.
Thus everything hangs in the branches, as there the me-nests stack
Idylls in the overcast evening. A contented dearth
With mists from the Last Days squats belly-down in the warmth.
Now flutes in the light in the dawn, as though a fragment of memory
Grows to remembrance down in the bedewed thicket. Saponify, saponify!
Quickly make of remembrance soap, through the scrub the gendarmes
With chains of flutes and tolling whips from east and west
Crack arse into belly into me-me-me, oh, forget, forget!
All around weathercocks clatter, shot-down names trail
Even in dying yet more spoor, as if they wanted to warn
The idylls in the branches above which, breathless and pressing
                                 together, want to reach
The Fourth Compassion be it as a letter of the alphabet or as a plague
                                     of such letters.

translated by Ken Cockburn | 1987

Die Heimat Nacht selbst aber schießt aus ihren Disteln und Farnen
Die Nester vom Geäst herunter. An beiden Armen
Aufgerissen im Arsch: landloses Begreifen

1987 | Robert Schindel

The ground of Night itself however shoots from its ferns and thistles
The nests out of the boughs. By both arms,
The shit worked out of you: realization of landlessness.

translated by Ken Cockburn | 1987

Drei Kugeln

1

Rund war der Kopf des Mannes vor der Tür, die
offen war; ein Mann, der weinte. Im Metzger-
laden lag ein Schweineschädel in der Sülze,
die schmackhaft aussah. Laß die Springflut
los, Wirt! Aus dem Rauch tauchen Arme. In der
Frühjahrswirtschaft brennt ein Berg mit roten
Zungen; durch die Wasserarme tauchen Finger,
die noch bluten. Vorne steht der Mann, der
heute weint. Leberblümchen wachsen an dem Riff.

Stetig brennen große Feuer, in den Nächten, die
von Hundsgekläff gut ausgefüllt sind. Schau nur
zu! Aus dem Innern kommt nichts, nur Rauch. Auf
den andern Bergen liegen andre um die Feuer, sie
feuern gut. Nur das weite Land ist verdunkelt.

2

Drüben stand das Haus; mit den Traufen, mit den
Rauchwimpeln hings nur lose in dem Morgen, der
grade erst gefügt war. Helle Stangen steckten
um den Baum im Schnee, zierlich war der Baum,
mit graden Ästen, die er streckte, daß die Vögel
kommen, gehen konnten; außerhalb war vieles noch.

In den Armen klang die Kälte von der Nacht, an der
breit geschwungnen Straße trug sie ihre Lampen
aus; rund war der große Lampenkopf. Hinten an
der Rampe putzten Männer an den Kannen, blank
warn einige schon, vor dem Wagen standen sie, sei–
ne Deichsel zeigte steil, schief zum Scheunentor.

3

Für die große Not gibts einen Abtritt, rechter-
hand vom Gang, dort hängt der Spiegelglanz.

1988 | Peter Rosei

Three Globes

1
Round was the head of the man beside the door, which
was open; a man who wept. In the butcher's
shop a pig's skull lay in brawn,
which looked delectable. Unleash the spring-tide,
landlord! Out of the smoke emerge arms. In the
hostelry of spring a mountain burns with red
tongues; through the arms of water emerge still-bleeding
fingers. There at the front is the man who
today is weeping. Liverwort grows on the reef.

Great fires burn steadily in the nights, well
filled with the yapping of dogs. Just look!
From the interior comes nothing, merely smoke. On
the other mountains others lie around the fire, they
fire well. Only the surrounding land is in darkness.

2
The house stood over there: with its eaves, with its
pennants of smoke it hung limp in the morning that
had just been uttered. Bright poles were stuck
around the tree in the snow, the tree was delicate,
with straight branches which it extended so the birds
could come, could go; without, there was much else besides.

The cold of the night tingled in the limbs,
laying out its lanterns by the road's broad curve;
round was the head of the great lantern. Behind on
the ramp men polished the canisters, some
were shining already, they stood before the cart, its
shafts pointing sheer and steep at the barn door.

3
In case of emergency there is an exit, to the right of
the corridor, where the gleaming mirror hangs.

translated by Ken Cockburn | 1988

Fest, mit beiden Händen, zeichnen die Verzwei-
felten ihre Urteilssprüche an die Wand; oder,
was nicht selten vorkommt, einen guten Witz.
Dann das Pissoir, wo die Riesen mit den Wasser-
fallen stehen, oft zu Eis gefroren: diese
Katarakte! Oben schwimmt der Rauch durchs Trink-
lokal, während an den Tischen, die recht klein
und abgeschunden in der großen Ferne stehn, sich
das kugelrunde Leben einen Scherz erlaubt: Bier
und Schweinebraten! An der Budel ragt der Kopf
des Königs fast zerplatzend in die Höhe; einsam
ist die rote Kugel. Bis die Glocke wieder tönt,
und die Tür Willkommen schwingt. Ja: Das Gassen-
fenster ist vom Nebel fein beschlagen, der sich
zaubrisch durch die Stadtluft wälzt; es schneit
ein wenig: Jetzt! Durch das Gassenfenster schaut
der Blinde, dann sein Freund, sein Schäferhund.

1988 | Peter Rosei

Firmly, with both hands, those in despair
inscribe their verdicts on the wall; or,
not infrequently, a good joke.
Then the urinal, where the giants stand with water-
falls, often frozen solid; those
cataracts! Above, the smoke swims through the bar,
while at the tables, which stand diminished
and knackered in the far distance,
barrel-shaped life allows itself a laugh: beer
and roast pork! At the bar the king's head
soars up fit to burst into the air: the red ball is
lonely. Till once again the bell chimes,
and the door waves a welcome. Yes: the street-
window is slightly misted over, by the mist which
waltzes like magic through the city air: it's snowing
a little: Now! Through the street-window
the blind man looks, and then his friend, his sheepdog.

translated by Ken Cockburn | 1988

velden

ein dunkler thonetstuhl am strand
einsam sechzigjährig gediegen
die grenze des panamahutes gut
vor die flimmernden augen gezogen
verschiedene charakteristika die
auf belesene vormittage hinweisen
ein japanischer lackkasten etwa
der abgerutschte seidenschal im gras
schriftstellerische betätigung ist
nicht unbedingt auszuschließen
sollte es aber schönberg sein er
der milchflaschen mit runden kieseln
mit geschossen seiner musik bewirft
wer tippt dann diese sonnenkringel
und die hellen mädchenkleider so
unablässig in die kühle olympia?

1989 | H.C. Artmann

velden

a thonet chair at the edge of the lake
dark-stained lonely sixty solid
the brim of the panama hat is pulled
down low before eyes that are restless
a range of characteristics which
are indicative of bookish mornings
a Japanese lacquer box say
a silken shawl discarded on the grass
authorial activity
cannot entirely be discounted
should however it be schoenberg he
who at milk-bottles directs pebbles
and his musical artillery
then who head-down insists on typing
these dazzling reflections and the bright
girls' dresses into the cool olympia?

translated by Ken Cockburn | 1989

Bajalice

moja pesem, kakor da ne bi bila od človeka, s prosojnimi stebri jezika, ki
preprečujejo, kar se je zdavanaj zgodilo. zakaj no obupujem, ne opupujem
več, kot bi želela, brezdanje, vsezazrto! ni več besed v meso zagozdenih, ne
brazgotin razbolelih. semena pogina bajajo, se sprijemajo, a ne iztečejo.

in vendar je jezik ves slutnja, z davno tesnobo zatohlih izb, polten,
kiselkast kakor groza pred smrtjo, trzanje praznih želodov, ki utihne.
je zvok, ki ga aroganca stvarnika nič več ne more presajati, le
zapisuje, kdaj se mu kakor materija v dlani razklene v propad.

kaj reči o pijanem telesu in zgrbljenem nosu, ki se v kot tišči,
ko pa vse ne bi smelo obstajati. skrb, ki glavo zastrupi, da se
potem pregiba in pljuje in kolne. kaj govoriti o neznosni
sopari, senenem drobu, volčjaku, ki neprestano meča liže. a

kadar so dnevi zlate svetlobne pošasti, se gibamo s trudno in
topo strastjo. meni se blede od vonja po senu, plemenu, da si
na čelo prvinsko čudenje rišem. z bregov grem od romanticizmov
v krvi zeleni, ki samo skrivoma rdi. čas rušilnih namenov je.

je prepadenost umišljena, je obvezna posledica samevanja? v njej
nikdar celote, sami obroki in spomini, ki se jih niti ne drznem
dotakniti, četudi so moji. med črke odlagam prepovedane radosti,
da neizrekljivo in sramno hirajo. vidno oksidiram, ustvarjam

šelest. vozli uma preskakujejo v pisane clip monsters
in odmor zgodnjih dni nepreklicno fiksira izhod. z nekaj
prebliski zasvedram navzgor in navzdol. kost raste.
ne da bi bila z njim, eden trdi, da ga ljubim. res je.

Divining

My song as though from somewhere else insists, a history
transport of transparent stumps. Better abandon better unlearn
the endlessly picked over long ago yearned for vegetable
word-cyst rooted in flesh, the unwithered alien integer.

It's close as intuition, a stilled vibration in the husk
a sour fall in empty rooms, familiar as the fear of death.
The sound, the yet unwritten, the thing that cannot find
a home, the split, the nearly immaterial thing.

No word for the crumpled nose, the sodden body corner-bent
as though its being were forbidden. No word for anxiety
to raze the head, to spit upon. No word for heavy heat, for
flung chaff, for slobber of the feral cub. Giant brightness

brings golden days, joys approach wearily and out of focus.
The hay sways with sex, I imprint amazement on my face.
I leave the hills and the green blood of my Romanticism
that has secretively reddened. It's time to go wrecking.

Is upheaval summoned up, or a consequence of loneliness?
There's no whole to it, just memories and guessing, barely
trustable even if mine. Between these marks I lay the prohibited
to waste away wordlessly in shame. And I oxidise. I create

murmurs. The mental tangle flattens into cartoon smash and grab
and a remembered serenity indicates the getaway. One or two
lightnings flicker me up and down. There's a bone growing.
I've never been with him but someone says I love him. It's true.

translated from the Slovenian by Angus Reid | 1990

Für Zoe

Auf dem Hügel warst du,
an einem Sommertag,
ringsum wies alles über sich fort,
woher Licht und Wind strömten,

Apfelbäume, überladen mit Wachstum,
standen am Abhang, eine Katze war es,
die dir glich, du lagst im Gras,
wohlvorbereitet war dein Rücken,
er hob sich für unsere Lust,

auch das Maisfeld hielt zu uns,
sein Grün machte den Himmel blau,
und der Blumenduft ließ dich duften,

die Worte waren verflogen,
was uns umschloß, war unsehbar nahe,
greifbar in dir als erster Gedanke,
als leerer, der uns zurückhielt
und forttrug.

1991 | Alfred Kolleritsch

For Zoë

You were out on the hill
that summer's day
and all around was pointing away
to wind and light instreaming –

apple trees, heavy with growth
standing on the slope, a cat,
like you, stretched in the grass,
your back, more than ready,
rising to pleasure us both –

the cornfield stood by us too,
its green turning sky to blue
and scent of flowers scenting you –

and all our words were gone,
while what held us was invisibly close,
palpable in you as a thought, beginning,
empty, holding us back
and carrying us away.

translated by Iain Galbraith | 1991

tigerpapier

aus den trümmern allen schäumens
solcher gischt von fetzen
hebt sich der löwe des bedeutens,
schüttelt seine mähne
—pflanzen, wörter, glück—und
heiter, mit der ganzen pracht der angst,
mit der ganzen wucht der wut,
brüllt er, schifft und vögelt
(möve seines besten stücks),
zerknüllt sich funkelnd so in jede beute,
speit auch schön, was gutes er hier tut,
schneidet schliesslich
—lamm des eigenen begreifens—sich
in streifen und zerspringt
mit diesem satz nach allen seiten:

1992 | Franz Josef Czernin

tigerpaper

from the rubble of what froths up
O such a spray of bits and pieces
the lion of meaning rises up,
shakes out his mane
—plants, words, happiness—and
blithely, with all the splendour of anxiety,
with the full force of fury, he
roars, has a slash, knocks one off
(he do the walk and do the talk!),
crumples—sparks flying—into prey
while spouting out the good he's doing,
ultimately scissors himself
—lamb of his self-reflexive grasping—
into strips and bounds
with this phrase in all directions:

translated by Iain Bamforth | 1992

Mitten im Land

Von den über Hänge
gestrafften Wiesen
gleiten und in
Getreidefeldern
wälzen sich Wind
und Windeskinder
Dort steh ich
dich seh ich
Herzschlag in meiner Zunge

1993 | Christoph Wilhelm Aigner

In the Middle of the Country

Down the slope-
stretched meadows
the wind and the wind's
children glide and go
tumbling in
cornfields
There I stand
you I see
heartbeat in my tongue

translated by Ron Butlin and Regi Claire | 1993

'schließlich & endlich das'

schließlich & endlich das
eins zwei drei vier fünf
eins zwei drei vier fünf finger
schließlich eins zwei drei

der böse & der gute finger die
böse & die gute hand & endlich
die zweite hand gut & böse
& schließlich & endlich die hände

eins zwei drei vier letzten endes
wo steckt der finger eins &
wo steckt der finger zwei &
schließlich & endlich die hand

letzten endes gut & böse drei vier
gut & böse fünf steckt der finger sechs
wo steckt er & schließlich wo
auf der hand sieben acht

neun zehn elf letzten endes
eins zwei drei vier fünf
finger suchen finger suchen
finger & die guten & die bösen

schließlich & endlichesuchen
wo steckt der finger & die hand
letzten endes suchen & finden
& finden & suchen eins & zwei

drei & vier fünf & sechs alle
finger sind schon da alle
finger alle stecken & finden
wo finden gut & böse wo

1994 | Reinhard Priessnitz

'finally & at last this'

finally & at last this
one two three four five
one two three four five fingers
finally one two three

the evil finger & the good the
evil hand & the good & finally
the second hand good & evil
& finally & at last the hands

one two three four at the last count
where is finger one hiding &
where is finger two hiding &
finally & at last the hand

at the last count good & evil three four
good & evil five is the finger hiding six
where is it hiding & finally where
in the hand seven eight

nine ten eleven at the last count
one two three four five
seeking fingers fingers seeking
fingers & the good ones & the evil

finally & seeking at last
where is the finger hiding & the hand
at the last count seeking & finding
& finding & seeking one & two

three & four five & six all the
fingers are now here all the
fingers are all hiding & finding
where to find good & evil where

translated by Ken Cockburn | 1994

findet die hand eine hand
meine hand deine hand
schließlich & endlich
böses suchen & gutes finden

letzten endes eins & zwei
drei vier fünf sechs & sieben

1994 | Reinhard Priessnitz

does the hand find a hand
my hand your hand
finally & at last
seeking evil & finding good

at the last count one & two
three four five six & seven

translated by Ken Cockburn | 1994

Bergtour und Ekelsuppe

Plötzlich ist Mama wieder aus dem Spital, wo sie todkrank lag. Wir betreten eine lang nicht mehr erlebte Landschaft: in viel düsterem Grün den steilen kurvigen Weg zu einem Hügel; der Weg wird sich zu einer Bergtour verlängern. Wir beide, sagen wir, können nicht mehr wie früher da hinauf. Aber für drei Stationen, jeweils Beuge in eine neue Richtung, reichts noch. Da sind wir in einem Berggasthaus, sollen uns mit einer Speise stärken. Die ist eine ganz unmögliche Suppe, wässerig, nicht gebunden, mit zerkochten großen Blättern drin, säuerlich-schal, Geruch wie von Nasen-Eiter bei Erkältung oder von Staub im Sauger, so auch der Geschmack beim ersten widerstrebenden Löffeln. Die Speise ist aber nicht verdorben sondern Landsbrauch. An den ich mich wohl nie gewöhnen werde. Ich entschließe mich, um Kräfte zu sammeln, Vorurteile sein zu lassen, halte mich aber an die einzig gewohnten – wenn auch zu wenig garen – Bohnen, die am Rand des Gebräus schwimmen. Glücklich bin ich in dieser neuen Umgebung nicht.

1995 | Andreas Okopenko

Mountains and Vile Soup

Suddenly mama's out of hospital again, where she lay at death's door. We're walking in a landscape we haven't trodden for ages: amid dense and gloomy foliage a steep winding path to a hill; the path will continue up into the mountains. Neither of us, we say, can make it up there now like we once could. But for three stretches, each veering in a different direction, It's still manageable. Then we're in a mountain inn, to keep our strength up with something to eat – a frankly impossible soup, watery, lacking body, with large overcooked leaves in it, stale and bitter, smelling of the kind of phlegm that accompanies a cold or like dust in a hoover, and that's how it tastes when I take my first reluctant spoonful. The food however isn't off but rather a speciality from hereabouts. Which I don't think I will ever get used to. I decide, in order to regain my strength, to set prejudice aside, but stick only to what's familiar, albeit undercooked, that is, beans, swimming at the edge of the broth. These new surroundings don't exactly fill me with joy.

translated by Ken Cockburn | 1995

Versöhnung

Weinen will ich meinen, Flachs und Schnee
die Hand dir zum Verstehen, Wintersaat
zu geben, was es eben nötig hat, du bist
mir all die Weile im Versteck, das heißt,
nicht vom Vertrauen weg. Scherensprüche,
braune Überreste, was weilend unter Lebenden
der November sonst zu schreien hat, das
nimmst du weg, Chiantiflasche, knappe Not,
ziehst keine Nummer, wie es Schleifer tun,
ab auch kein Vertun. Du Sein im Heiligen,
im lange her, sogar die Bäume,
paradiesisch nackt, wollen, wie ich weiter meine,
zum Ende nichts mehr tun. Diesmal,
mehr nicht nötig haben wir, wird kund
und wahr die Botschaft sein. Die Liebe,
diese sieht wie langes Alter aus und
daher will ich weinen meinen, Flachs und Schnee.

1996 | Franzobel

Reconciliation

Weeping I should say so, flax and snow
to give you my hand in understanding, seedplants
for winter, whatever's called for, you're mine
though you stay in hiding, in other words,
not forsaking trust. Cutting talk,
brown residues, what November, tarrying among
the living, otherwise has to shout about, that
you take away, Chianti bottle, close shaves,
don't pull a number like the grinders do,
no losing the plot either. You being in sanctity,
survivor of the calendar, even the trees,
naked as in the Garden, desire, I mean to add,
non-activity when they're through. This time
we need for nothing more, the message
will be loud and clear. This thing called love
looks like protracted ageing and that's
why I should say so weeping, flax and snow.

translated by Iain Bamforth | 1996

Physikalische Optik I

er kam aus dem november · der hagel brachte
    ihn herab · all das wasser auf den flügeln
die nähte und die grate einer gußform

    die im regen hing bis der wind sie kappte
und er dann an die scheibe schlug wie ein bügel
    der aus seinem schloß schnappt · der ahorn

dort und seine äste · so schwarz war er
    eisengrau der bauch · nur ein paar federn
zum schwanz hin heller doch kaum scheinbarer

    als seine schwere nun plötzlich am balkon
in die sich die krallen hakten · norwegen
    oder die tundra · kein anderes land dachte

ich mir ließ diese tarnung zu und dem schnabel
    nach zu schließen war es wohl ein sperling
augen dunkel wie mangan und ein ring

    ganz weiß und schmal fast wie abgeschabt
von diesem schauen · flüsse im winter wegwärts
    ein erzeinschluß in den pupillen · das herz

ein flacher kiesel unter hagelschlossen
    zurückgelegt in den oktober · aufgehoben
war er leicht und das wort »vogel« eine vokabel

unklarer herkunft und von irgendwo im norden

innsbruck, 22. 10. 96

1997 | Raoul Schrott

Physical Optics I

it came out of november · the hail brought
    it down · all that water on the wings
the seams and fins of a cast

    that hung in the rain till cut by the wind
it struck against the pane like a shackle
    snapped from a lock · that maple

there and its branches · it was that black
    its breast iron grey · a few feathers brighter
towards the tail though hardly more apparent

    on the balcony now than this sudden gravity
its claws still clung to · norway
    or the tundra · no other land i thought

could warrant this disguise and judging
    by the beak it had to be a sparrow
eyes dark as manganese and a ring

    pure white and small as if scraped thin
by all that looking · rivers in winter along the way
    inclusions of ore in the pupils · its heart

a flat pebble among the hailstones
    handed back to october · picked up it felt
light and »bird« a word of obscure

origin and from somewhere in the north

innsbruck, 22. 10. 96

translated by Iain Galbraith | 1997

'Obstbaumblüte zwischen Sträuchern'

Obstbaumblüte zwischen Sträuchern
Mauern, in Zeilen und Feldern mit
Gärten, Schuppen, Birken, ewiges
Ziehen, Wolken und Blätter, es
waren Dörfer, Stunden, Namen

Kam und an, bemoost, verrußt, war
Schweiß und Schlaf und stand als
einer, der steht bei seiner Tasche im
Staub, es summte, etwas verloren
sangen ein paar Vögel, welches

Wort, frage ich, würde das erste hier
sein, oder rauchte, schaute und die
örtliche Straße entlang, wo kein
Mensch nur war, die Blumen im
Schotter wankten, bewegt von

Weither, Wissen, Ziegel, Ödnis, es
war, gehörte ich der Ödnis, dem
Morgen, er säumte mit Gräsern die
Beete, die aufgebrochen lagen, von
Wicken überwachsen, umflort

1998 | Michael Donhauser

'Fruit tree blossom between bushes'

Fruit tree blossom between bushes
walls, in rows and fields with
gardens, sheds, birches, unending
passage, clouds and leaves, there
were villages, hours, names

Arrived and there, mossy, dark with
soot, was sweat and sleep and stood
as one who stands beside his bag in the
dust, there was humming, a few
birds singing a bit forlorn, which

Word, I asked, would be the first
here, or smoking looked, and
along the main street, where no
person was, only flowers in
the gravel swayed, troubled from

Afar, knowing, bricks, lost land
it was I belonged to the lost land, the
morning, fringing with grasses the
beds, which lay there broken up
grown over with vetch, wreathed

translated by Iain Galbraith | 1998

'Ich zum Beispiel war schon Knabe, Mädchen, Pflanze'

Ich zum Beispiel war schon Knabe, Mädchen, Pflanze,
Vogel und Flut-enttauchender Fisch. Ich war erhaben
wie eine Zeder redete und wie eine Zypresse Zahn-
ragt in Alleen, flammend von Efeu und Phlox. Ich
war als eine Palme Hand-handelte, und als eine Rose
Oleander, der Ölbaum auf dem Feld, Anger und
Lilien, die silbern, Libellen, sind. Ich verströmte das
Aroma der Herbeiche, Ahorn und Holunder, Strauch-
Zimt und Minze von Asphalt, Platanen, Myrizen die-

die Tamarinden von Halbhölzern, Rhododendrien die
Harz-Narden und Rebrohr Astern die Scharlachbeeren
Gallapfel und Geißfeig-Wespen, Seckelklee und Weber-
kardel Hagebuch, die Linden, Pappeln, Nadelblumen
Jade und Laubzierraten, Mistel-fach, um 'eines Tages,
vielleicht sehr bald schon' spaltbreit (in allem, was wir
tote Natur nennen) dieses Land-in-sich zusehends *zu sein*.

1999 | Oswald Egger

'I for instance have been lad, girl, plant'

I for instance have been lad, girl, plant,
bird and fish leaping the rapids. I was exalted
like a cedar spoke and like a cypress jutted
dental in avenues flaming with ivy and phlox. I
was like a palm-tree hand-handling, and like a rose
oleander, the olive-tree in the field, village green and
lilies, which are silver, dragonflies. I exuded the
smell of dry oak, maple and elderberry, cinnamon
bush and mint of asphalt, plane-trees, tamarisks which-

the tamarinds of half-woods, rhododendrons the
resinous valerian and vine-tubes asters scarlet-berries
oak gall and caprifig-wasps, purse-clover and weaver's-
teasel hornbeam, the lindens, poplars, needle-flowers
jade and ornamental foliage, mistletoe-fold, 'one day,
perhaps very soon', through a fissure (in everything we
call inert nature) *to be* this country as it constitutes.

translated by Iain Bamforth | 1999

manu scriptum oder
der hufeisengewinn

(nach Ossip Mandelstam)

es schreibt der ruck
so kräftig, drückt,
dass glückt dem arm,
was streich der hand

–das bleibt,
nicht für sich selbst, es schreibt
des griffels zeichen ein,
auf wand, die zeigt,
wo so gehautes treibt

wie:
»hirnenmund«
– der sperrt sich auf –
verbeisst sich nichts,
gibt kunde, auch wenns pecht
schürft er die ecke rund
– schwatzt ab, was juckt ihn, laut
das murmeln schluckt den ton,
hebt ab so alles
stimmige im fluss

(wird span des griffels, feder – nun im sprung)

– begriffen stirn wie stein,
herz wie holz,
im hinten denkt sich
noch ein druck was aus:
die form –
eisen, schirmt nicht ab,
es bildet lieber aus den tritt
als ein, was sich so normt
verliert es gern –

2000 | Ferdinand Schmatz

manu scriptum or
the horse-shoe gain

(after Osip Mandelstam)

a lurch, it writes,
its surge robust,
to urge the arm
to tryst the wrist

– it stands
not for itself, inscribes
the pencil's hand
on the wall, which bends
the gaze to where such scorings branch

like:
'mouth of brains'
– which gapes –
keeps nothing down,
makes known, under a cloud
scrapes corners round
– coaxes the itch, loud,
the murmurings surround its tone,
thus in the flux
the canorous resounds

(becomes slate-pencil, sliver-quill – darting now)

– as head and lead
heart and slate,
behind, another press
thinks something up:
its form –
an iron, does not screen,
but rather shapes than dreams
the fall of foot, such norms as grow
is glad to forgo –

translated by Iain Galbraith | 2000

was aus spricht nur,
sich mustert im spalier

dort, wo es fliesst:
ein bild aus silben, lauten
nächtens

(traum, gefärbt)

gibt wild sich hin
bis in den tag, der wird gesetzt
in schrift

(nicht hin gefetzt, die sprach' ein schild)

höchstens
stosst sie hand
wetzt den finger übers jetzt

– das donnert in der stille auf,
und steht dann drauf, verbrieft
dass nimmer eingebrannt das glück,
nie stück wird, sondern lauf

(der ziechen kreis fliegt taubend auf)

und kreidet an, was bleich
an worten bloss
von der blüten stil sich löst

2000 | Ferdinand Schmatz

whatever just opines
and keeps itself in line

but when it flows:
an image made of syllables and sounds
nightlong

(dream, in colours)

giving itself in furious abandon
until day comes, which then
is set in script

(not scribbled, language a shield)

at most
hustling the hand
finger-skimming over the now

– in the stillness thunders
then is done, a bond that states
bliss is no longer branded,
no piece-work that, but run

(the letters' circle, dove-winged, rises)

and chalks out what – so pale
in words – has merely
loosed itself from flowery style

translated by Iain Galbraith | 2000

Verbindungsbahn

Als die drei Schwestern vom Ball nach Hause kamen, war der Vater tot. Am Morgen half es nichts mehr, die Waggons der Lastzüge zu zählen. Wenig später wurde auch das Kaffeehaus im unteren Stockwerk aufgelassen und der Garten von den Gartenstühlen geräumt. Was blieb, war die Schnapsboutique auf der anderen Seite der Bahn, der Schirmladen und das Kloster, das keine Novizinnen nahm. Sie verließen die Schule.

Aber heute noch grüßen die grünen Bäume über die Mauer, die Blätter, durch die man wie durch Trompten blasen kann. Der Maiwind wiegt den schwarzen Rauch und zerstreut ihn. Bei der italienischen Botschaft biegen Kinder ein, kurz darauf erscheinen weiße Wolken am Himmel. Mit einer Verheißung beginnt der Nachmittag.

Wer geht vor dem Abend noch einmal über den Steg und bläst das Lied durch die Blätter? Wer hilft die Wagen zählen und stellt die Gartenstühle wieder in den Rauch? Von der Kasernenkirche läuten jetzt die Glocken. Der Mond ist im Kommen. Mit einer Frage beginnt die Nacht.

2001 | Ilse Aichinger

Connecting Train

When the three sisters came home from the ball, their father was dead. Next morning, it no longer helped to count the wagons of the freight trains. A little later the coffee house on the lower floor was closed down, too, and the garden cleared of garden chairs. What remained was the off-licence on the other side of the tracks, the umbrella shop and the nunnery that didn't take novices. They left school.

But even today the green trees give their greeting across the wall; the leaves through which you can blow as if through trumpets. The May wind sways the black smoke, scattering it. Children turn off into the Italian Embassy; shortly afterwards white clouds appear in the sky. The afternoon begins with a promise.

Who will cross the footbridge once more before evening and blow the song through the leaves? Who will help to count the wagons, and set the garden chairs out again in the smoke? The bells are ringing from the barracks' church. The moon is rising. The night begins with a question.

translated by Ron Butlin and Regi Claire | 2001

»Dearest be cheerful«

Als ich meine Brille abnahm
Mir die Finger an die Schatten
Unter meinen Augen legte
Erschrak ich über die Sanftheit
Mit der ich mich berührte

Meine Finger gehörten einem Wesen
Aus einer Welt mit anderen Maßen
Es war meine oftmals ausgeführte
Geste aber enthoben ihrer Schwere
Fähig nur zum Echo eines Drucks

Mein Schrecken nahm sich zurück
Zu einem vorsichtigen Wundern
Über meine Finger und ihren Auftrag
Mir eine Nachricht zu überbringen
Aus einem anderen klügeren Körper

Ich sollte etwas lernen aber was es
War zeigte sich noch nicht
Es zögerte als gehörte das dazu
In diesen sich öffnenden Sekunden
In denen Platz für das Fremde war

Dann entstieg ich dem Moment
Der mit mir innegehalten hatte
Und ich wußte es war der Nachklang
Deiner leichten Worte gewesen
Die ich gerade überdacht hatte

2002 | Evelyn Schlag

'Dearest be cheerful'

When I took off my spectacles
Put my fingers to the shadows
Under my eyes
I was shocked at the gentleness
With which I touched myself

My fingers belonged to a being
From a world with different measures
It was an often-performed
Gesture but relieved of its weight
Capable only of the echo of a pressure

My shock gave way
To a cautious wondering
About my fingers and their task
To convey a message to me
From another more knowledgeable body

I was meant to learn something but what it
Was didn't yet show itself
It hesitated as if that was to be expected
In these unfolding seconds
In which there was room for the unusual

Then I stepped out of the moment
That had paused with me
And I knew I had felt the resonance
Of your casual words
That I had been thinking over

translated by Ron Butlin and Regi Claire | 2002

Notes on the Poems

1978:   Readers of the German poem will notice an apparently anomalous instance of capitalization at the beginning of line 16. This follows the authority of *Sämtliche Gedichte* (1978), as the first book publication of 'Böhmen liegt am Meer'. Subsequent printings of the poem in 1993 (*Werkausgabe*) and 2002 (*Sämtliche Gedichte*, 2nd edition) have retained the capitalization. Consultation of Bachmann's typescripts (reproduced in *Letzte, unveröffentlichte Gedichte, Entwürfe und Fassungen*. Edition und Kommentar von Hans Höller, 1998) reveals her handwritten insertion of the majuscule in the final stages of composition as well as its retention in a subsequent typescript in which Bachmann gave detailed attention to orthography. Perhaps this explains why successive editors have tended to view the present reading as not only anomalous but intentional.

1979:   'eller', a Norwegian word meaning 'or'; 'afers': a valley and settlement near nobert c. kaser's native Brixen.

1981:   'angel esterminador': (Spanish, 's'-spelling of 'esterminador' is obsolete and dialect) exterminating angel.

1984:   words in italics in the translation mark English inclusions in the German text;. 'puigcerda': a mountain border town between the Catalan province of Girona and France.

1989:   'velden': a small town on the north bank of the Wörthersee, a lake in Carinthia, Austria; 'thonet chair': the Viennese company founded by the furniture manufacturer Michael Thonet (1796-1871) produced the famous curvilinear 'Chair 14', which sold some 40 million copies between 1856 and 1939.

1994:   I am indebted for his advice to Ferdinand Schmatz, General Editor of the *Werkausgabe* of Reinhard Priessnitz's writings, from which 'schließlich und endlich das' is reprinted, and to Thomas Eder (University of Vienna) for providing a copy of Priessnitz's typescript of the poem (unpublished in his lifetime), allowing me to confirm the poet's use of what might otherwise take the appearance of an editorial oversight: the word 'endlichesuchen' in line 21.

Biographies and Acknowledgements

The Editors

Volume Editor:

IAIN GALBRAITH was born in Glasgow and grew up in Arrochar, Loch Long. He studied Modern and Medieval Languages at Cambridge, German Studies at the University of Freiburg, and Comparative Literature at the University of Mainz, where he taught for several years. He has edited writing by Robert Louis Stevenson, James Hogg, James Boswell, Joseph Conrad and Walter Scott for a classics series, and has contributed essays to many literary and cultural journals and books in the United Kingdom, Germany and France. His German versions of British and Irish plays have been performed at more than a hundred theatres in Germany, Austria and Switzerland, and he is also a widely-published translator of German-language writing – especially poetry – into English, winning the John Dryden Prize for Literary Translation in 2004. His own poetry has appeared in numerous anthologies and journals, including the *TLS*, *New Writing*, *Best Scottish Poems 2005*, *New Writing Scotland*, *PN Review* and *The Allotment: New Lyric Poets* (2006). His recent book publications include – as editor – *Intime Weiten. XXV Schottische Gedichte* (2006) and *Michael Hamburger: Pro Domo. Selbstauskünfte, Rückblicke und andere Prosa* (2007), and he is the translator of *Alfred Kolleritsch: Selected Poems* and *Peter Waterhouse: Selected Poems*, both to appear in 2007.

Series Editor:

ROBYN MARSACK was born and grew up in Wellington, New Zealand, and holds a BA from Victoria University, a B. Phil. and D. Phil. from Oxford. She worked with Carcanet Press between 1982 and 1987, first as Editorial Manager and later as a Director. In 1987 she moved to Scotland, working as a freelance editor, translator from French, and critic, reviewing poetry regularly for Scottish newspapers. In 2000 she was appointed Director of the Scottish Poetry Library in Edinburgh. She lives in Glasgow. Her published work includes *The Cave of Making: Poetry of Louis MacNeice* (1985), Nicolas Bouvier: *The Scorpion Fish* (translator, 1987), *Sylvia Plath* (1992), Nicolas Bouvier: *The Way of the World* (translator, 1997), Nina Berberova: *Aleksandr Blok: A Life* (translator, 1996), and *Intimate Expanses, XXV Scottish Poems, 1978-2002* (co-editor, 2004).

Poets' Biographies
with sources for the poems

ILSE AICHINGER, 1921–

Born in Vienna, her family were persecuted as Jews under National Socialism, her grandmother and an aunt deported to their deaths in 1942. In 1947 she interrupted her medical studies to complete her novel *Die größere Hoffnung*/The Greater Hope (1948), to this day one of the most widely read post-war novels in the German language. In 1952 – a year before her marriage to the poet Günter Eich – she was awarded the prestigious Literature Prize of 'Group 47'. Following sojourns in several parts of Austria and Germany she returned to Vienna in 1988. She has published novels, radio plays, stories, poetry and prose poems, and an edition of her works in eight volumes appeared in 1991. Among her prizes are the Petrarca Prize (1982), and the Great Austrian State Prize (1995) for her life's work. The volume *Kurzschlüsse. Wien*/Short Circuits. Vienna (2001) contains prose poems written between 1953-55, each the touchstone of a Viennese topography of loss. In English: *Selected Poetry and Prose,* translated by Allen H. Chappel (Durango, Colorado: Logbridge-Rhodes, 1983).

,Verbindungsbahn', in *Kurzschlüsse. Wien*. Herausgegeben und mit einem Nachwort von Simone Fässler (Wien: Edition Korrespondenzen, 2001) © Ilse Aichinger & Edition Korrespondenzen, Vienna 2001

CHRISTOPH WILHELM AIGNER, 1954–

Born in Wels, Upper Austria, he studied German and Sport in Salzburg, where he worked 1979-84 on the editorial staff of the newspaper *Salzburger Tagesblatt*. He became a freelance author in 1985 and lived for many years in Salzburg. He has won numerous awards, including the Anton Wildgans Prize (2004) and the Great Austrian State Prize for Literature (2006). He is a translator of Guiseppe Ungaretti (*Zeitspuren*, 2003), and his books of poetry include *Weiterleben*/Living On (1988), *Landsolo*/Land Solo (1993), *Das Verneinen der Pendeluhr*/The Negation of the Pendulum Clock (1996), *Die Berührung*/Touched (1998), *Vom Schwimmen im Glück*/On Bathing in Happiness (2001), and *Kurze Geschichte vom ersten Verliebtsein*/Short History of First Being in Love (2005). His intense, imagistic lyrics are at their strongest where natural landscapes listen to the human heart. He lives in Italy.

,Mitten im Land', in *Landsolo* (Salzburg: Otto Müller Verlag, 1993) © Christoph Wilhelm Aigner

H. C. ARTMANN, 1921–2000

A master of masks and legerdemain in biographical matters (a practice defended on the grounds of being a poet), Artmann wrote under several pseudonyms and in several 'imagined' languages, including 'Pictish'. Probably born in Breitensee, on the outskirts of Vienna, he travelled widely and translated from English, Danish, French, Dutch, Spanish and Swedish, from which – collector and exhibitor of words that he was – he translated the botanist and zoologist Carl von Linné's Lappland diary. The son of a cobbler, he left school to work in an office. Called up in 1940, injured in 1941, he repeatedly attempted to desert, and was interned by the Americans in 1945. His first poems, collected some 20 years later in *ein lilienweißer brief aus lincolnshire*/a lily-white letter from lincolnshire (1969), were broadcast by Radio Vienna in 1947. He was an early member of the Vienna Group of language-artists in 1953, and the author of a great variety of work in different genres, including dialect poetry and children's verse. He received many prizes, including Germany's most prestigious award, the Georg Büchner Prize. He moved to Salzburg in 1972 and died in Vienna in 2000. His *Sämtliche Gedichte*/Complete Poems appeared in 2003. In English: *The Quest for Doctor U.*, translated by Malcolm Green and Derek Wynand (London: Atlas Press, 1993). 'Blind Chance and Roast Duck', translated by Malcolm Green, in *Beneath Dark Stars*, edited by Martin Chalmers (London: Serpents Tail, 2002).

‚velden', in *Sämtliche Gedichte* (Salzburg und Wien: Jung und Jung, 2003). Originally in: *gedichte von der wollust des dichtens in worte gefaßt* (Salzburg und Wien: Residenz, 1989) © Jung und Jung 2003, Salzburg und Wien

INGEBORG BACHMANN, 1926–1973

Born in Klagenfurt, Carinthia, Bachmann is one of Austria's foremost twentieth-century writers and one of the most influential post-war poets in the German language. After concluding her studies with a doctorate on the philosophy of Martin Heidegger in 1950, she worked as a radio journalist in Vienna before rocketing to prominence as a poet at a meeting of 'Group 47' in 1952, winning the Group's prestigious prize in 1953. She lived mainly in Rome from 1953 until her untimely death there in 1973, and her two volumes of poetry, *Die gestundete Zeit*/Borrowed Time (1953) and *Anrufung des Großen Bären*/Invocation of the Great Bear (1956) were received to rapturous critical acclaim. It has been maintained that Bachmann fell silent as a poet in the late fifties, focusing thenceforward exclusively on fiction and radio plays, and collaborating with the composer Hans Werner Henze, but posthumous publications of her poetry render this thesis at least questionable. The cycle of poems to which 'Böhmen liegt am Meer' ('Bohemia, a Country by the Sea') belongs was begun in Prague in 1964, after a traumatic stay in Berlin. Bachmann won many prizes, including the Georg Büchner Prize (1964) and the Great Austrian State Prize for Literature (1968). In English: *Darkness Spoken: The Collected Poems of Ingeborg Bachmann*, translated by Peter Filkins (Brookline/M.A.: Zephyr Press, 2006); *Last Living Words: The Ingeborg Bachmann Reader*, translated by Lilian M. Friedberg (Los Angeles: Green Integer, 2006).

,Böhmen liegt am Meer', in *Sämtliche Gedichte* (München: Piper Verlag, 1978) © Piper Verlag GmbH, München 1978, 2002

Franz Josef Czernin, 1952–

Born in Vienna, now lives in Rettenegg (Styria). He studied in the USA in the early 1970s, returning to lecture at Indiana University in 1988. A forceful sense of poetic accountability combined with an intense critical awareness of tradition and experiment imbues his work in every field, and in 1980 he began his 'Kunst des Dichtens' (Poetic Arts), an artwork of encyclopaedic scope, integrating essays, poetic forms and even software design. His accolades include the Vienna Literary Prize (1997) and the Heimito von Doderer Prize for Literature (1998). Among his many published works are a volume of translations of Shakespeare's sonnets (1999), volumes of his own sonnets, including *elemente. sonette/ elements. sonnets* (2002), essays on Hausmann, Kafka, Kraus, Musil and Trakl, and his book-length dialogic, epistolary and aphoristic interrogations of poetic *topoi* and forms.

,tigerpapier', in *Gedichte* (Graz: Literaturverlag Droschl, 1992) © Literaturverlag Droschl, Graz-Wien 1992

Michael Donhauser, 1956–

Born in Vaduz (Liechtenstein), has lived in Vienna since 1976. Donhauser is a master of the miniature, a precise annalist of 'outdoor' sensory experience, a celebrator of synaesthetic disturbance. He has published several acclaimed volumes of poetry, short prose, a novel, and the volume of essays *Vom Sehen*/On Seeing (2004). He has translated poetry by Arthur Rimbaud and Francis Ponge, and is the recipient of a number of prestigious prizes, including the Meran Poetry Prize (2004) and the Ernst Jandl Prize for Poetry (2005). His work includes the volumes *Von den Dingen*/About Things (1993), *Siebzehn Diptychen in Prosa*/Seventeen Diptychs in Prose (2002), *Vom Schnee*/On Snow (2005) and his selected poems *Ich habe lange nicht doch nur an dich gedacht*/For a long time I did not think but only of you (2005).

,Obstbaumblüte zwischen Sträuchern', in *Sarganserland* (Basel/Weil am Rhein/Wien: Urs Engeler Editor, 1998) © 1998 Urs Engeler Editor, Basel, Weil am Rhein, Wien. 'Fruit tree blossom between bushes' first appeared in: *Shearsman*, No. 57, 2003/2004.

Oswald Egger, 1963–

Grew up in Lana, South Tyrol, where he has continued to live. He concluded his studies in Vienna with a dissertation on hermetic poetics. From 1989 to 1998 he edited the magazine *Der Prokurist*, and has recently been a guest writer at Hombroich Island/Germany, Villa Aurora/Los Angeles, and Cornell University/Ithaca. Prizes for his work include the Clemens Brentano Award (2000) and Meran Poetry Prize (2002). He has collaborated with several composers, especially with Michael Pisaro, who published English versions of Egger's work in *Room of Rumor. Tunings* (2004). Egger's poetry is an expression of extreme lexical vigilance, teaching us new ways of reading. In 1999, under the anagrammatic and probably untranslatable titles *Herde der Rede. Poem* and *Der Rede Dreh. Poemanderm Schlaf*, he published two parts of a poetic text of some 15,000 lines, a symphonic celebration of the word-hoard, warping and wefting the poetic and discursive, charting the sources and courses of the Hippocrene. Eggers most recent books are *Prosa Proserpina Prosa* (2004) and *Lustrationen*/Lustrations (2007).

,Ich zum Beispiel war schon Knabe, Mädchen, Pflanze', in *Herde der Rede. Poem* (Frankfurt/Main: Suhrkamp, 1999) © Suhrkamp Verlag Frankfurt am Main 1999

Franzobel, 1967–

Born as Stefan Griebl in Vöcklabruck, Upper Austria, he studied German and History in Vienna, while working as an extra at the Burgtheater and regularly showing his paintings. He took up writing in 1989 and is possibly Austria's most prolific living author, with some 40 books (many of them full-length works of prose fiction) and plays to his name in the past decade alone. He has won several prestigious prizes, including the Ingeborg Bachmann Prize (1995), but a less well-known prize, the Kassel Literature Prize for Grotesque Humour (1998), also speaks volumes. Much of his work is satirical, and he is a gifted writer for the stage. His poetry, whose ludic exuberance, like that of his prose, can recall Ringelnatz, Schwitters, Hausmann, Morgenstern or Jandl, makes up a relatively small part of his oeuvre. His recent work includes *Zirkusblut oder Ein Austrian-Psycho-Trashkrimi, zweiter Teil*/Circus Blood, or An Austrian Psycho Trash Thriller, Part Two (2005).

,Versöhnung', in *Luna Park. Vergnügungsgedichte* (Wien: Zsolnay, 2003); *Ringelspiel-Zyklus* (1996) © Paul Zsolnay Verlag Wien 2003

ERICH FRIED, 1921–1998
Born into a Viennese Jewish family, he went to school in Vienna, organizing a resistance group against the Nazis in 1938. His father died after a Gestapo interrogation, and Fried fled to London, where he lived until his death (in Baden-Baden) in 1998. From 1952 to 1968 he worked for the BBC, becoming a full-time writer in 1968. His early decision to resist oppression and defend human rights became inseparable from his impulse to write, and his politically engaged poetry is often mentioned in conjunction with Heine, Tucholsky or Brecht. His willingness to turn his poetry to political effect made him a literary figurehead on the political Left, especially in the late 1960s when his volume *und Vietnam und*/and Vietnam and (1966) reached a large and youthful readership. He published 45 volumes of poetry in his lifetime, among them the best-selling *Liebesgedichte*/Love Poems (1979), and was awarded many prizes, including the Carl von Ossietzky Medal (1986) and the Georg Büchner Prize (1987). He was a gifted translator of T.S. Eliot, Sylvia Plath, Dylan Thomas and Christopher Marlowe, and published German versions of 27 of Shakespeare's plays. His *Gesammelte Werke*/Collected Works were published in four volumes in 1993. In English: *100 Poems Without a Country* (New York: Red Dust Books, 1990); *Love Poems* (London: Calder Publications, 1991, 1999), both translated by Stuart Hood.

,Trakl-Haus, Salzburg', in *Das Nahe suchen* (Berlin: Verlag Klaus Wagenbach, 1982) © 1982, 1998 Verlag Klaus Wagenbach, Berlin

Maja Haderlap, 1961–

Born in Bad Eisenkappel/Železna Kapla, she attended the Federal Slovenian Grammar School and studied German and Theatre Studies in Vienna. After completing a doctorate in 1989 she was a junior lecturer in Comparative Literature at Klagenfurt University and worked as a theatre dramaturge and translator, becoming Senior Dramaturge at Klagenfurt Theatre in 1992. A long-serving editor of the Carinthian Slovenian literary and cultural journal *Mladje*, she has written poetry, criticism and radio plays, receiving a number of prizes for her work, including the France Prešeren Foundation Prize (1989) and the Hermann Lenz Prize Promotional Award (2004). Her volumes of poetry are *Žalik pesmi*/Blessed Poems (1983), *Bajalice*/Divining (1987), and a collected poems, with translations into German and English, entitled *Gedichte/Pesmi/Poems*, 1990-1995, in which her own German poems appear for the first time. Metaphors of exile and escape, arrival and hope fill her recent work, refusing circumscription, renegotiating borders.

,Bajalice', in *Österreichische Lyrik und kein Wort Deutsch*, herausgegeben von Gerald Nitsche (Innsbruck: Haymon Verlag, 1990) © Založba Drava, Klagenfurt/Celovec, 1998

Ernst Jandl, 1925–2000

Born in Vienna he studied German and English in Vienna, completing his studies in 1950 with a doctorate on the novellas of Arthur Schnitzler. He was a teacher until 1979, by which time he had already achieved international renown. A list of his publications, including poems, radio plays, theatre plays, libretti, film scripts, prose, essays, lectures and translations (e.g. Robert Creeley, John Cage, Gertrude Stein) would resemble the telephone book of a small town, and an edition of his poetic works alone was published in ten volumes in 1997. He received many prestigious prizes during his lifetime, including the Georg Büchner Prize (1984) and the Heinrich von Kleist Prize (1993). The titles of several of his books have become almost proverbial in German – *lechts und rinks*/reft and light (1995) coming immediately to mind – and he is remembered as much for the spellbinding acoustic feats of his readings, with audiences regularly in the hundreds, as for his published work. In English: *Dingfest – Thingsure*, translated by Michael Hamburger (revised edition, Dublin: Dedalus Press, 2006).

‚schweizer armeemesser', in *selbstporträt des schachspielers als trinkende uhr* (Darmstadt, Neuwied: Luchterhand Verlag, 1983) © Luchterhand Literaturverlag, München, 1983, 1997: einem Unternehmen der Verlagsgruppe Random House GmbH

Norbert C. Kaser, 1947–1978

Born in Brixen (South Tyrol), he grew up in a poor working-class family in Bruneck. In 1968 he entered a Capuchin monastery, leaving a year later to study Art History in Vienna. He visited Norway as a student worker in 1970, but left university prematurely in 1971, returning to South Tyrol, becoming a labourer and, in 1973, a village teacher. After a period in a psychiatric hospital in Verona in 1975, he joined the Italian Communist Party. His poems, short prose and letters are collected in three substantial volumes. Outside the small circle of his friends the importance of his writing remained largely unrecognised until after his early death. He always wrote his name in lower case, and this practice continues to be respected by his editors. His collected poems contain translations of work by Montale, Leopardi, Quasimodo, Fortini and Saba, as well as his own Italian poems. He died of a lung oedema and advanced liver cirrhosis in Bruneck in 1978.

‚die laerche', in *Gedichte. Gesammelte Werke – Band 1*, herausgegeben von Sigurd Paul Scheichl (Innsbruck: Haymon Verlag, 1988); first published in *Eingeklemmt*, Innsbruck: Edition Galerie Bloch, 1979) © Haymon-Verlag, Innsbruck-Wien, 1988, 1991

Marie-Thérèse Kerschbaumer, 1936–

Born in Garches/France to an Austrian mother and Cuban father, she spent her childhood in Costa Rica and Tyrol, moving to Vienna in 1957. She studied German, Roumanian and Italian, concluding her studies with a doctorate in 1973. She began writing in the 1960s, and besides translations from Spanish and Roumanian, has published poetry and fiction and written radio plays and film scripts, including a TV-adaptation of her documentary work *Der weibliche Name des Widerstands*/The Female Name of Resistance (1980), which follows the lives of seven women in their struggle against the Nazi regime. Much of her work has a political or utopian edge, drawn tautly between hope and disappointment. Her most recent books include *Wasser und Wind. Gedichte 1988-2005*/Water and Wind. Poems 1988-2005 (2006), the third part of the trilogy of novels *fern*/far away (2001), a book of essays entitled *Calypso. Über Welt, Kunst, Literatur*/Calypso. On the World, Art, Literature (2005) and *Neun Elegien*/Nine Elegies (with Spanish translations by Elena Maria Blanco, 2004). Among her accolades are the Meersburg Droste Prize (1985) and the Vienna Literary Prize (1995).

‚vierhundert kinder im schnee', in *bilder immermehr. gedichte 1964-1987* (Salzburg, Wien: Otto Müller Verlag, 1997) © 1997 Otto Müller Verlag Salzburg-Wien

Alfred Kolleritsch, 1931–

Born in Brunsee/Steiermark, he studied History and Philosophy at the University of Graz, where, in 1964, he defended a doctorate on the philosophy of Martin Heidegger. He taught in a grammar school in Graz from 1964 until 1993, and was a founder member of the Graz cultural centre 'Forum Stadtpark' in 1959, becoming its president in 1968, and a founder member of the Graz Authors' Association in 1973, to which he remained attached until 1983. He is editor of the influential literary magazine *manuskripte*, which he co-founded in 1960. His own work first appeared in 1958, and he has since published poetry, as well as novels, film scripts, radio texts and children's books. His many poetry collections include two retrospective selections, in *Gedichte*/Poems (1988) and *Die Verschwörung der Wörter*/The Conspiracy of Words (2001). He has been awarded several prizes for his work, including the Georg Trakl Prize for Poetry (1987) and the Horst Bienek Prize (2005). In English: *Selected Poems*, translated by Iain Galbraith (Exeter: Shearsman Books, 2007).

‚Für Zoe', in *Gegenwege* (Salzburg: Residenz Verlag, 1991) © Literaturverlag Droschl, Graz-Wien

Friederike Mayröcker, 1924–

Born in Vienna, where she lives today. From 1946 to 1969 she taught English at Viennese secondary schools. In 1954 she met the poet Ernst Jandl and maintained a close literary and personal partnership with him until his death in 2000. Her first book appeared in 1956, and she left teaching to become a full-time writer in 1969, publishing poetry, prose work, radio plays, children's stories, texts for the stage and film scripts. Among her many prizes are the Friedrich Hölderlin Prize (1993) and the Georg Büchner Prize (2001). Her prose work (1949-2001), often associative and poetic in character, is collected in five volumes. Besides more than 80 book publications she has continued to be a highly influential presence (as a poet rather than essayist or reviewer) in literary magazines. Her uniquely synthetic collage compositions have fascinated critics and poets alike, and her example has inspired an uniquely broad constituency of younger writers, including Thomas Kling and Marcel Beyer, the latter editing her *Gesammelte Gedichte 1939-2003*/Collected Poems (2004). In English: *Raving Language: Selected Poems 1946-2005*, translated by Richard Dove (Manchester: Carcanet, 2007).

,von damals an', in *Gesammelte Gedichte 1939-2003*. Herausgegeben von Marcel Beyer (Frankfurt/Main: Suhrkamp, 2004); date of composition 26.1.1980 © Suhrkamp Verlag, Frankfurt am Main, 2004

Andreas Okopenko, 1930–

Born in Kosice (Slovakia), he moved to Vienna in 1939, where he still lives. He studied Chemistry at Vienna University and, while his poems had begun to appear in the late 1950s, worked in industry for many years before becoming a full-time writer in 1968. From 1950-1953 he was editor of the hectrographed literary journal *publikationen einer wiener gruppe junger autoren*/publications of a viennese group of young authors, which contained early work by Ernst Jandl, Friederike Mayröcker, H. C. Artmann and others. He has written poetry, novels and short prose, as well as plays for radio and stage and a film-script, and has received several prestigious prizes for his work, including the Great Austrian State Prize for Literature (1998) and the Georg Trakl Prize for Poetry (2002). Among his most well-known works is the formally innovative *Lexikon-Roman einer sentimentalen Reise zum Exporteur Treffen in Druden*/Lexicon-Novel of a Sentimental Journey to the Export Convention at Druden (1970), considered a classic of Austrian 'avant-garde' writing, and the partly autobiographical novel *Kindernazi*/Child Nazi (1984). His *Gesammelte Lyrik*/Collected Poems appeared in 1980 and his collected essays in two volumes in 2000 and 2001. In English: *Child Nazi*, translated by Michael Mitchell (Riverside, CA: Ariadne Press, 2003).

,bergtour und ekelsuppe', in *manuskripte* 129, vol. 35 (September 1995). Later in *Traumberichte* (Linz: Edition Blattwerk, 1998). © Andreas Okopenko

Heidi Pataki, 1940–2006

Born in Vienna, where she lived and worked all her life, studying

Journalism, History of Art and Economics at Vienna University, in 1970 becoming an editor of the Viennese monthly journal *Neues Forum*, and for 1981-83 editor of the Austrian film magazine *Filmschrift*. She was a journalist and broadcaster for Austrian radio for many years, also writing for radio stations in Germany as well as contributing to print media, including the Viennese newspaper *Die Presse* and the magazine *Jüdisches Echo*. In 1973 she was a founding member of the Graz Authors' Association, whose President she became in 1991. Her literary work consisted mainly of poetry and essays, many of her poems employing montage techniques with political and humane intention. Her collected poems appeared under the title *Amok and Koma. Gedichte aus dreißig Jahren*/Amok and Coma. Poems of Thirty Years (1999), while her volume of essays *Contrapost. Über Sprache, Kunst und Eros*/Contrapost. On Language, Art and Eros appeared in 2001. She received a number of awards for her work, including the Vienna Literature Prize (1998).

,angel esterminador', in *Neues Forum* 335/336 (1981) © Otto Müller Verlag 1999

Reinhard Priessnitz, 1945–1985

Born in Vienna where, with the exception of a period spent in Holland in 1953, he continued to live until his untimely death from cancer. He began writing and publishing his work while still at school, and although only one volume of poems appeared during his lifetime, *vierundvierzig gedichte*/forty-four poems (1978), his work became a gauge of poetic audacity for poets and critics, including Ferdinand Schmatz, Franz Josef Czernin and the young Thomas Kling. He was associated with Hermann Nitsch and the Vienna Actionist movement in 1965, and his work is often placed in the context of the 'experimental' Vienna Group and the international concrete poetry movement. In fact, such intellectual-aesthetic currents provided the backdrop against which Priessnitz generated his own eccentric and often unusually sensual poetics. Besides poetry he wrote essays (e.g. on Pound, Handke, Bernhard, Mayröcker) and short prose, and, from 1976 until his death, contributed regular reviews to the Viennese newspaper *Die Presse*. He also worked as an editor for various journals and publishers, including the Viennese cultural journal *Neues Forum* (1968-74), the *edition neue texte* (1976-83), and Medusa Verlag (1983-88). In 1973 he was a founding member of the Graz Authors' Association, and in 1982 held teaching posts at the Vienna Academy of the Fine Arts and the University of Arts and Industrial Design in Linz. After his death he was awarded the Austrian Appreciation Prize for Literature (1985). His collected works appeared in five volumes between 1986 and 1994, edited by Ferdinand Schmatz.

,schließlich und endlich das', in *Texte aus dem Nachlaß*. Herausgegeben von Ferdinand Schmatz (Graz und Wien: Literaturverlag Droschl, 1994). © Literaturverlag Droschl, Graz-Wien 1994

PETER ROSEI, 1946–

Born in Vienna, he studied Law at the University of Vienna, completing his studies with a doctorate in 1968. After a brief period as an art dealer and as secretary to the Viennese painter Ernst Fuchs, he took to full-time writing in 1972. His first book was a volume of stories, *Landstriche*/Pieces of Land (1972), and he has continued to publish novels and shorter fiction, as well as volumes of poetry, of which the most recent was *Viel früher*/Much earlier (1998), plays for radio and stage, essays and film scripts, including a co-translation of Michelangelo Antonioni's *Zabriskie Point*. He has been referred to as Austria's most restless writer, his journeys and places entering the fabric of his fiction and providing the subjects of his travel writing. He has received many prizes and awards, including the Franz Kafka Prize (1993) and the Vienna Literature Prize (1996). His most recent publication is the novel *Wien Metropolis*/Vienna Metropolis (2005). He lives in Vienna. In English: *Ruthless and Other Writing*, translated by Geoffrey Howes (Riverside/C.A.: Ariadne, 2003); 'Franz and I', translated by Michael Hofmann, in *Bananas*, Special German Number, December 1979.

,Drei Kugeln', in *Luchterhand Jahrbuch der Lyrik 1988/89*. Herausgegeben von Christoph Buchwald und Friederike Roth (Darmstadt: Luchterhand Literaturverlag, 1988) © Peter Rosei

ROBERT SCHINDEL, 1944–

Born in Bad Hall, near Linz, the son of Austrian Jewish communists who were deported to concentration camps, he was expelled from secondary school in Vienna, taking part-time jobs in Paris and Sweden, studying Law and Philosophy at Vienna University, involving himself in various communist groups and as spokesman of the Vienna Commune, a radical section of the late-1960s students' movement. After spells as a librarian and journalist, he became a freelance writer in 1986, publishing a novel, stories, poetry and scripts for radio, film and television. His many prizes include the Eduard Mörike Prize (2000) and the Jacob Wassermann Prize (2006), and his most recent books are a volume of essays *Mein liebster Feind*/My Favourite Enemy (2004), his collected poems *Fremd bei mir selbst*/Strange With Myself (2004) and a new collection *Wundwurzel*/Sore-Root (2005). In English: *Born-Where*, translated by Michael Roloff, (Riverside/C.A.: Ariadne, 1995); 'Clever Kids Die Young', translated by Iain Galbraith, in *Beneath the Stars. Contemporary Austrian Short Stories*, edited by Marin Chalmers (London: Serpent's Tail, 2002).

,Heimatromanze/oder/Friedenslitanei Heimat Nacht Natur/ (Pour Hölderlin 11)', in *Geier sind pünktliche Tiere* (Frankfurt/Main: Suhrkamp, 1987) © Suhrkamp Verlag Frankfurt am Main 2004

Evelyn Schlag, 1952–

Born in Waidhofen an der Ybbs, where she lives today, she studied English and German in Vienna and worked for many years as a teacher at the Federal Academy of Trade and Industry in her native town. She has written poetry, novels, stories and essays, for which she has won prizes and awards, among them the Anton Wildgans Prize (1997) and the Otto Stoessel Prize (1998). Her poems address the intensity and fragility of happiness, and the ever-present threat of loss and pain. She has translated several poets from English, notably Douglas Dunn's *Elegies*. Her poetry includes *Das Talent meiner Frau*/My Wife's Talent (1999) and *Brauchst du den Schlaf dieser Nacht*/Do You Need This Night's Sleep (2002), and her most recent novels are *Das L in Laura*/The L in Laura (2003) and *Architektur einer Liebe*/Architecture of a Love (2006). In English: *Selected Poems*, translated by Karen Leeder (Manchester: Carcanet, 2004).

,'Dearest be cheerful'', in *Brauchst du den Schlaf dieser Nacht* (Vienna: Paul Zsolnay Verlag, 2002) © Paul Zsolnay Verlag Wien 2002

Ferdinand Schmatz, 1953–

Born in Korneuburg (Lower Austria), he now lives in Vienna, where he studied German, History and Philosophy. His work as a teacher at a number of universities has initiated interdisciplinary investigation into the uses and interfaces of writing and the other graphic arts, while his own writing has often been seen in terms of the Viennese tradition of 'experimental' language-criticism. His texts can be read as an aural decoding of the roots and links of poetic speech and thought. He has written a novel (*Portiersch*, 2001), radio plays and several volumes of essays, but is best-known as a composer of poetic texts, such as *Das große Babel,n/*The Great Bab(ble)/ (el) (1999). Among the many prizes he has received for his work are the Austrian State Prize for Literature (2001) and H. C. Artmann Prize for Poetry (2006).

,manu scriptum oder der hufeisengewinn', in *manuskripte* 150, Jg. 40 (November 2000). Later in: *Tokyo, Echo oder wir bauen den Schacht zu Babel, weiter* (Innsbruck: Haymon, 2004) © Haymon-Verlag, Innsbruck-Wien, 2004

RAOUL SCHROTT, 1964–

Born in 1964, he grew up in Tunis and Tyrol, later studying in Paris, Berlin, Innsbruck, Norwich and Naples. He now lives in Ireland, and has won many important prizes for his work, including the Leonce and Lena Prize (1995) and the Peter Huchel Prize (1999). He has written novels, stories and film scripts, and his best-known books of poetry are *Hotels* (1995), *Tropen. Über das Erhabene/*Tropes-Tropics. On the Sublime (1998), and *Weißbuch/*White Book (2004). He first became known as a 'reinventor' of the poetic canon with his anthology of translations *Die Erfindung der Poesie. Gedichte aus den ersten viertausend Jahren /*The Invention of Poetry. Poetry of the First Four-Thousand Years (1997), and his own poetry and fictions also express a restless concern with myth and source, complementarity and parallax. In English: *The Lob Nor Desert*, translated by Karen Leeder (London: Picador, 2002).

,Physikalische Optik I', in *Tropen. Über das Erhabene* (München: Hanser Verlag, 1998) © 1998 Carl Hanser Verlag München Wien. First published in: *Sinn und Form*, Jg. 49, Heft 2, März/April 1997. 'Physical Optics I' appeared first in: *Stand*, Vol. 1, No. 4, December 1999.

JULIAN SCHUTTING, 1937–

Born (as Jutta Schutting) in Amstetten, Lower Austria, he trained as a photographer at the College of Graphic Arts before going on to study History and German at the University of Vienna, concluding his studies with a doctorate in the history of law. In 1965 he became a teacher at a Technical College, later becoming a full-time writer. His writing includes poetry, essays, radio plays, shorter and longer prose, and he has received numerous prizes, including the Anton Wildgans Prize (1983) and

Georg Trakl Prize for Poetry (1989). His volumes of poetry include *In der Sprache der Inseln*/In the Language of the Isles (1973), *Lichtungen*/Glades (1976), *Traumreden*/Dreamtalk (1987), *Das Eisherz sprengen*/Blasting the Ice-Heart (1996) and *Dem Erinnern entrissen*/Torn from Oblivion (2001). Commentators have noticed an unusual cryptic or elliptical quality in Schutting's poetry, a shift to parataxis and the fragmentary. Such characteristics are anything but rare in contemporary poetry, however, and it is in the lyric as much as anywhere that Schutting excels. His best work sings; unrestricted by the Parnassian, it is deft and touching.

‚Salerno', in *Traumreden* (Salzburg: Residenz Verlag, 1987). First published in *Luchterhand Jahrbuch der Lyrik 1985*. Herausgegeben von Christoph Buchwald und Ursula Krechel (Darmstadt: Hermann Luchterhand Verlag, 1985) © Julian Schutting

PETER WATERHOUSE, 1956–

Born in Berlin, has lived in Vienna since 1975. He studied English, German and Philosophy in Vienna and Los Angeles, completing a doctorate on Paul Celan in 1984. He has written poetry, essays, prose and drama, and his translations from English and Italian (especially the multi-volume editions of Andrea Zanzotto and Michael Hamburger) are undertaken in the spirit of an ongoing poetic research project, developed in essays, discussions, poems. He has won many prizes for his work, including the Münster Prize for European Poetry (1993) and the Austrian State Prize for Literary Translation (2002). Among his volumes of poetry are *Menz* (1984), *Passim* (1985) and *Prosperos Land* (2000). His most recent work is the genre-defying memoir-fiction *(Krieg und Welt)*/(War and World) (2006), which, like much of his work, elicits new strategies for reading and inward listening. In English: *Where are we now?* translated by Rosmarie Waldrop (Sausalito: Duration Press, 1999), and *Selected Poems*, translated by Iain Galbraith (Exeter: Shearsman, 2007).

‚Hauptstadt der Sprache', in *passim. Gedichte* (Reinbek bei Hamburg: Rowohlt, 1986) © Urs Engeler Editor, Basel, Weil am Rhein und Wien 2001

Translators' Biographies

IAIN BAMFORTH, 1959–
Born in Bishop's Stortford, he grew up in Glasgow, where he studied Medicine at the University. Since 1995 he has lived in Strasbourg, where he ran a medical practice. He has travelled widely both within and outwith Europe, and makes regular sorties as a doctor to South East Asia. He has contributed to a wide range of cultural and literary journals, including the *Times Literary Supplement*, *London Review of Books* and *New York Times Book Review*, and his volumes of poetry include *Sons and Pioneers* (1992), *Open Workings* (1996) and *A Place in the World* (2005). He is the editor of the anthology *The Body in the Library. A Literary History of Modern Medicine* (2003), and his own recent book of essays is *The Good European. Arguments, Excursions and Disquisitions on the Theme of Europe* (2006).

RON BUTLIN, 1949–
Born in Edinburgh, where he lives with his wife, the writer Regi Claire. He has published novels, short stories, poetry, radio plays and libretti, and his poetry and fiction have won several Scottish Arts Council Book Awards and a Poetry Book Society Recommendation. His work has been translated into over a dozen languages, and the French edition of his novel *The Sound of My Voice* won the Prix Millepages 2004 and the Prix Lucioles 2005 (both for Best Foreign Novel). His work has been included in many anthologies, including *New Writing*, and *The Faber Book of 20th Century Scottish Poetry*, and he has been commissioned to write libretti and poem-sequences for the BBC Scottish Symphony, the Scottish Chamber Orchestra, the Hebrides Ensemble and the Edinburgh String Quartet, among others. He has been Writer-in Residence at the universities of Edinburgh, Stirling, St. Andrews and New Brunswick. His most recent publications include the novel *Belonging* (2006) and *Without a Backward Glance: new and selected poems* (2005).

REGI CLAIRE, 1962–
Born and brought up in Thurgau canton, Switzerland, studied English and German at the University of Zurich and Aberdeen. English is her fourth language. She moved to Britain in 1993 and now lives in Edinburgh with her husband, the poet and novelist Ron Butlin. She was awarded the Saltire First Book Award for her first volume of short stories, *Inside-Outside* (1999), while her first novel, *The Beauty Room* (2002), was

longlisted for the Allen Lane/MIND Book of the Year Award. She won the Edinburgh Review 10th Anniversary Short Story Competition and was a major prizewinner in the Cadenza International Short Story Competition. She has recently completed a new novel, 'Women without Men', and is currently finishing another collection of stories, 'Fighting It'. Her work has been translated into several languages and broadcast on BBC Radio 4.

Ken Cockburn, 1960–

Born in Kirkaldy, he studied French and German at Cardiff and worked from 1996 to 2004 as Fieldworker and Assistant Director at the Scottish Poetry Library. He now lives as a freelance poet, editor and writing tutor in Edinburgh. His first collection of poems, *Souvenirs and Homelands*, was shortlisted for a Saltire Award in 1998, and his work has appeared in several anthologies, including *Dream State: The New Scottish Poets* (2nd edition, 2002). With Alec Finlay, he established pocketbooks, an award-winning series of books of poetry and visual art, and among the works he has edited are *The Jewel Box. Contemporary Scottish Poems*, Audio-CD (2000), *The Order of Things: Scottish Sound, Pattern and Concrete Poems* (2001), *Intimate Expanses: XXV Scottish Poems 1978-2002* (2004) and *The Season Sweetens/Die Saison versüssend: Football Haiku*, 2006. His translations of German-language poetry include work by Arne Rautenberg and Rudolf Bussmann.

Iain Galbraith, 1956–
See editors.

Angus Reid, 1966–

Born in Oxford, grew up in Edinburgh. He spent ten years living in Slovenia and now lives in Edinburgh again. His theatre plays *How to Kill*, *The Trouble with the Dead* and *Believer* all won awards at the Edinburgh Festival Fringe in the 1990s. His film work includes *Brotherly Love* (1994) and *The Ring* (2004), the latter receiving the prize for the Best Central European Documentary Film 2004 at the Jihalva International Documentary Film Festival. His first collection of poetry *The Gift* was published in 2001, followed by *White Medicine* in 2004.

Acknowledgements

Other XXV Anthologies

Intimate Expanses
XXV Scottish Poems 1978-2002

Edited by Ken Cockburn and Robyn Marsack

This anthology of 25 Scottish poems, one from each year from 1978 to 2002, presents an alternative view of how the past quarter century has unfolded in Scotland. These poems document history in small things as well as grand gestures, and range from sonnets and haiku to gargantuan list-poems.

The poets included are Iain Bamforth, Meg Bateman, John Burnside, Robert Crawford, Carol Ann Duffy, Douglas Dunn, Gerrie Fellows, Robin Fulton, Andrew Greig, George Campbell Hay, W.N. Herbert, Kathleen Jamie, Tom Leonard, Liz Lochhead, Norman MacCaig, Aonghas Macneacail, Kevin MacNeil, Edwin Morgan, Don Paterson, Richard Price, Seán Rafferty, Alastair Reid, Iain Crichton Smith, Alan Spence, Gael Turnbull.

'As this anthology begins in the year of MacDiarmid's death, it seems appropriate to open not with a poem by the old poet, but with a poem about the death of the father. Alastair Reid's touching, personal poem concludes not with an ending but a beginning, of 'that hesistant conversation /which will go on and on'. Indirectly all the writers of this quarter century are linked to MacDiarmid, in the sense that he provided the model of a poet questioning issues of identity, politics, culture, metaphysics and language within this shared geography which we call Scotland.'

from the Introduction by Ken Cockburn

ISBN 1 85754 795 0, December 2004, £7.95

At the End of the Broken Bridge
XXV Hungarian Poems 1978-2002

Edited by István Turczi and with an Introduction by Béla Pomogáts

István Turczi, with his wife Anna Palos Turczi, runs the publishing house Parnasszus, producing a quarterly literary magazine of the same name, as well books by contemporary Hungarian poets, translators and essayists. He is also a poet, novelist, dramatist and translator.

A number of poets in this volume will be familiar to Anglophone poetry-lovers, such as Ágnes Nemes Nagy, Ottó Orbán and Sándor Weöres, while others are being translated for the first time.

The poets included are István Baka, Zsófia Balla, Lászlo Benjamin, Győző Csorba, György Faludy, Győző Ferencz, Ágnes Gergely, Gyula Illyés, László Kálnoky, István Kemény, Endre Kukorelly, Lászlo Lator, Ágnes Nemes Nagy, Ottó Orbán, György Petri, Sándor Rákos, Zsuzsa Rakovszky, Zsuzsa Takács, Dezső Tandori, János Térey, Krisztina Tóth, István Turczi, Szabolcs Várady, István Vas, Sándor Weöres.

The poems have been translated into English and Scots by Ron Butlin, Tom Hubbard, Edwin Morgan, Angus Reid and Christopher Whyte. Zsuzsanna Varga has acted as literary consultant for the anthology.

'These twenty-five poems reflect the psychological history of those twenty-five years. They reflect the thoughts and feelings of Hungarian poetry about a historical period suffused with historical change. I am certain that the task of providing an authoritative picture of the history of a human community and a European nation is too important to be left to the hard (or even the softer) sciences alone: I believe it to be an important task of poetry. It is in this sense that the poems in the anthology can be seen to provide valuable and reliable insights into the mental and psychological history of Hungarians in the twentieth and twenty-first centuries.'

from the Introduction by Béla Pomogáts

ISBN 1 85754 796 9, April 2005, £7.95

How to Address the Fog
XXV Finnish Poems 1978-2002

Edited by Anni Sumari

This anthology of 25 Finnish poems, one from each year from 1978 to 2002, presents an alternative view of how the past quarter century has unfolded in Finland. 'I took it as my aim to make the selection as elegant (read: readable and suitably rough) and interesting as possible, rather than being faithful to "archaeological" layers – and that was all.' The poems include examples of Finnish modernism, prose poems, aphoristic pieces, and writing in Finland-Swedish.

The poets included are Kari Aronpuro, Bo Carpelan, Tua Forsström, Paavo Haavikko, Anne Hänninen, Hannu Helin, Markku Into, Eeva Kilpi, Eila Kivikk'aho, Juhani Koskinen, Jarkko Laine, Rakel Liehu, Arto Melleri, Lassi Nummi, Lauri Otonkoski, Markku Paasonen, Mirkka Rekola, Pentti Saarikoski, Helena Sinervo, Eira Stenberg, Anni Sumari, Arja Tiainen, Sirkka Turkka, Gösta Ågren; and the translators Donald Adamson, Robin Fulton and David McDuff.

'You have in your hands an anthology of Finnish poetry covering a period of 25 years (1978–2002). It begins with a wild prose poem experiment by Sirkka Turkka (b. 1939) – a text of four pages. Perhaps surprisingly, the prose poem is one of the central trends in contemporary Finnish poetry. It's a genre that has been practised intensively for several decades, yet typically its practitioners are often lyrical poets, not prose writers. One main reason for the strength of the prose poem may be the nature of the Finnish language: the words are relatively long, and numerous inflections are added on at the end of words. The language's very structure encourages both the prose poem and the long, prose-like stanza, which has recently been an equally strong stylistic genre. On the other hand, Finnish is adept at yielding neologisms whose associative and auditory qualities seem natural to the reader and are easily understood.'

from the Introduction by Anni Sumari

ISBN 1 85754 816 7, February 2005, £7.95